The Politics and Pragmatics of Institutional Research

James W. Firnberg, William F. Lasher, *Editors*

NEW DIRECTIONS FOR INSTITUTIONAL RESEARCH
Sponsored by the Association for Institutional Research
MARVIN W. PETERSON, *Editor-in-Chief*
PATRICK T. TERENZINI, *Associate Editor*

Number 38, June 1983

Paperback sourcebooks in
The Jossey-Bass Higher Education Series

Jossey-Bass Inc., Publishers
San Francisco • Washington • London

James W. Firnberg, William F. Lasher (Eds.).
The Politics and Pragmatics of Institutional Research.
New Directions for Institutional Research, no. 38.
Volume X, number 2.
San Francisco: Jossey-Bass, 1983

New Directions for Institutional Research Series
Marvin W. Peterson, *Editor-in-Chief,* Patrick T. Terenzini, *Associate Editor*

Copyright © 1983 by Jossey-Bass Inc., Publishers
and
Jossey-Bass Limited

Copyright under International, Pan American, and Universal Copyright Conventions. All rights reserved. No part of this issue may be reproduced in any form — except for brief quotation (not to exceed 500 words) in a review or professional work — without permission in writing from the publishers.

New Directions for Institutional Research (publication number USPS 098-830) is published quarterly by Jossey-Bass Inc., Publishers, and is sponsored by the Association for Institutional Research. The volume and issue numbers above are included for the convenience of libraries. Second-class postage rates paid at San Francisco, California, and at additional mailing offices.

Correspondence:
Subscriptions, single-issue orders, change of address notices, undelivered copies, and other correspondence should be sent to *New Directions* Subscriptions, Jossey-Bass Inc., Publishers, 433 California Street, San Francisco, California 94104.

Editorial correspondence should be sent to the Editor-in-Chief, Marvin W. Peterson, Center for the Study of Higher Education, University of Michigan, Ann Arbor, Michigan 48109, or Patrick T. Terenzini, Office of Institutional Research, SUNY, Albany, New York 12222.

Library of Congress Catalogue Card Number LC 82-84192

International Standard Serial Number ISSN 0271-0579

International Standard Book Number ISBN 87589-956-0

Cover art by Willi Baum

Manufactured in the United States of America

Ordering Information

The paperback sourcebooks listed below are published quarterly and can be ordered either by subscription or single-copy.

Subscriptions cost $35.00 per year for institutions, agencies, and libraries. Individuals can subscribe at the special rate of $21.00 per year *if payment is by personal check*. (Note that the full rate of $35.00 applies if payment is by institutional check, even if the subscription is designated for an individual.) Standing orders are accepted. Subscriptions normally begin with the first of the four sourcebooks in the current publication year of the series. When ordering, please indicate if you prefer your subscription to begin with the first issue of the *coming* year.

Single copies are available at $7.95 when payment accompanies order, and *all single-copy orders under $25.00 must include payment*. (California, New Jersey, New York, and Washington, D.C. residents please include appropriate sales tax.) For billed orders, cost per copy is $7.95 plus postage and handling. (Prices subject to change without notice.)

Bulk orders (ten or more copies) of any individual sourcebook are available at the following discounted prices: 10–49 copies, $7.15 each; 50–100 copies, $6.35 each; over 100 copies, *inquire*. Sales tax and postage and handling charges apply as for single copy orders.

To ensure correct and prompt delivery, all orders must give either the *name of an individual* or an *official purchase order number*. Please submit your order as follows:

Subscriptions: specify series and year subscription is to begin.
Single Copies: specify sourcebook code (such as, IR8) and first two words of title.

Mail orders for United States and Possessions, Latin America, Canada, Japan, Australia, and New Zealand to:
    Jossey-Bass Inc., Publishers
    433 California Street
    San Francisco, California 94104

Mail orders for all other parts of the world to:
    Jossey-Bass Limited
    28 Banner Street
    London EC1Y 8QE

New Directions for Institutional Research Series
Marvin W. Peterson, *Editor-in-Chief*
Patrick T. Terenzini, *Associate Editor*

IR1 *Evaluating Institutions for Accountability,* Howard R. Bowen
IR2 *Assessing Faculty Effort,* James I. Doi
IR3 *Toward Affirmative Action,* Lucy W. Sells
IR4 *Organizing Nontraditional Study,* Samuel Baskin

IR5   *Evaluating Statewide Boards,* Robert O. Berdahl
IR6   *Assuring Academic Progress Without Growth,* Allan M. Cartter
IR7   *Responding to Changing Human Resource Needs,* Paul Heist, Jonathan R. Warren
IR8   *Measuring and Increasing Academic Productivity,* Robert A. Wallhaus
IR9   *Assessing Computer-Based System Models,* Thomas R. Mason
IR10 *Examining Departmental Management,* James Smart, James Montgomery
IR11 *Allocating Resources Among Departments,* Paul L. Dressel,
      Lou Anna Kimsey Simon
IR12 *Benefiting from Interinstitutional Research,* Marvin W. Peterson
IR13 *Applying Analytic Methods to Planning and Management,* David S. P. Hopkins,
      Roger G. Schroeder
IR14 *Protecting Individual Rights to Privacy in Higher Education,* Alton L. Taylor
IR15 *Appraising Information Needs of Decision Makers,* Carl R. Adams
IR16 *Increasing the Public Accountability of Higher Education,* John K. Folger
IR17 *Analyzing and Constructing Cost,* Meredith A. Gonyea
IR18 *Employing Part-Time Faculty,* David W. Leslie
IR19 *Using Goals in Research and Planning,* Robert Fenske
IR20 *Evaluating Faculty Performance and Vitality,* Wayne C. Kirschling
IR21 *Developing a Total Marketing Plan,* John A. Lucas
IR22 *Examining New Trends in Administrative Computing,* E. Michael Staman
IR23 *Professional Development for Institutional Research,* Robert G. Cope
IR24 *Planning Rational Retrenchment,* Alfred L. Cooke
IR25 *The Impact of Student Financial Aid on Institutions,* Joe B. Henry
IR26 *The Autonomy of Public Colleges,* Paul L. Dressel
IR27 *Academic Program Evaluation,* Eugene C. Craven
IR28 *Academic Planning for the 1980s,* Richard B. Heydinger
IR29 *Institutional Assessment for Self-Improvement,* Richard I. Miller
IR30 *Coping with Faculty Reduction,* Stephen R. Hample
IR31 *Evaluation of Management and Planning Systems,* Nick L. Poulton
IR32 *Increasing the Use of Program Evaluation,* Jack Lindquist
IR33 *Effective Planned Change Strategies,* G. Melvin Hipps
IR34 *Qualitative Methods for Institutional Research,* Eileen Kuhns, S. V. Martorana
IR35 *Information Technology: Advances and Applications,* Bernard Sheehan
IR36 *Studying Student Attrition,* Ernest T. Pascarella
IR37 *Using Research for Strategic Planning,* Norman P. Uhl

Contents

Editors' Notes 1
James W. Firnberg, William F. Lasher

Chapter 1. The Pragmatic Imperative of Institutional Research 3
William L. Tetlow

The effective communication of desired information between the generator and the user requires one to accommodate variances in decision-making style, behavior, and decision context.

Chapter 2. The Politics of Information 11
Cameron L. Fincher

If knowledge is power, and humans are political animals, the politics of information is undoubtedly what institutional research and management in the 1980s are all about.

Chapter 3. Politics Within the Institution 25
Laura E. Saunders

The institutional researcher needs to understand the political setting in order to ensure that institutional research is influential and becomes the basis for action.

Chapter 4. The Politics of Comparing Data with Other Institutions 39
Deborah J. Teeter

Data from other institutions provide management the ability to size up the competition, benchmarks for assessing the well-being of their own institution, the ability to pinpoint areas deserving attention, and guides for policy development.

Chapter 5. The Politics of Dealing with State Agencies — An Institutional View 49
E. Grady Bogue

A condescending attitude on the part of campus executives and their staff toward state agency staff is less likely to contribute to good relationships than mutual respect.

Chapter 6. Institutional Research and State Government — A State Agency View 63
Paul E. Lingenfelter

Institutional researchers influence state government decisions through their information and analysis and their interpersonal skills.

Chapter 7. Institutional Research, Politics, and 77
the Federal Government
John Folger
The federal government's role in the support of educational research and statistics useful for institutional research is reviewed, and the uncertain prospects for the future are assessed.

Chapter 8. The Future of Institutional Research 89
William F. Lasher, James W. Firnberg
Previous discussion is synthesized. The role of institutional research in higher education today and its future course are discussed.

Index 101

The Association for Institutional Research was created in 1966 to benefit, assist, and advance research leading to improved understanding, planning, and operation of institutions of higher education. Publication policy is set by its Publications Board.

PUBLICATIONS BOARD
Marilyn McCoy (Chairperson), University of Colorado System
Daniel R. Coleman, University of Central Florida
Jean J. Endo, University of Colorado-Boulder
William P. Fenstemacher, University of Massachusetts-Boston
Horace F. Griffitts, Tarrant County Community College District
Richard B. Heydinger, University of Minnesota

EX-OFFICIO MEMBERS OF THE PUBLICATIONS BOARD
Charles F. Elton, University of Kentucky
Richard R. Perry, University of Toledo
Marvin W. Peterson, University of Michigan

EDITORIAL ADVISORY BOARD
All members of the Publications Board and:
Frederick E. Balderston, University of California, Berkeley
Howard R. Bowen, Claremont Graduate School
Roberta D. Brown, Arkansas College
Lyman A. Glenny, University of California, Berkeley
David S. P. Hopkins, Stanford University
Roger G. Schroeder, University of Minnesota
Robert J. Silverman, Ohio State University
Martin A. Trow, University of California, Berkeley

Editors' Notes

In reality, politics is an important element in everyone's life. In our society, individuals, groups, and organizations constantly compete for influence and power. One definition of politics provided by Webster's is "the art or science of guiding or influencing the setting of policy." By this definition, individuals, groups, and organizations are actively engaged in political activities.

This is true for institutions of higher education as well as in the field of institutional research (IR). Of course, there may be differences in degree. Institutional researchers who approach their responsibilities as academic pursuits will probably be less involved in politics than will colleagues who focus on administrative and policy issues. The former, the classic researcher, emphasizes such things as theoretical studies of the internal dynamics of institutions of higher learning, the effectiveness of an institution's academic program, and the long-term impact of higher education on students. The latter focuses on information and studies that support decisions concerning current and future institutional policies and procedures, such as enrollment forecasts, cost analyses, faculty productivity, and so on.

Nevertheless, many institutional researchers deny that politics affects them. They consider the political arena to be dirty or sinister—something to be avoided. But because all relationships in our society are, in some sense, political, politics neither can nor should be avoided.

The purpose of this sourcebook is to explore the interrelationships between institutional research and the politics of higher education. The editors have approached this subject by providing two rather general discussions about the nature of institutional research and of information itself, followed by five chapters each of which deals with politics at a particular level within the organizational hierarchy of higher education. The volume concludes with a discussion of what the future may hold for institutional research.

The authors are particularly suited to discuss their various topics because of their backgrounds and experiences. William L. Tetlow has written extensively on the history and nature of institutional research. He has held institutional research positions at two major institutions and has recently moved to the National Center for Higher Education Management Systems. Cameron L. Fincher has been a faculty member studying higher education for many years. His discussion of the politics of information should be of interest to those who believe an institutional researcher's world is always rational. Laura E. Saunders has held institutional research positions in several institutions. She discusses how an IR office can best fit into an institution's organizational structure. Deborah J. Teeter has had a great deal of experience with interinstitutional information exchanges. E. Grady Bogue is currently a university president, but he used to be a state agency staff member. This experience on both sides of the coordination fence has given him valuable insights. Paul E. Lingenfelter is a state agency staff member. He argues that institutional researchers should influence state government decisions through their interpersonal skills as well as their information and analysis. John Folger has worked on and written about institutional, state, regional, and federal higher education problems for many years. He discusses the role of institutional research at the federal level.

The editors thank these individuals for sharing their expertise with us. The politics of higher education and of institutional research are rarely discussed, and are written about even less often. This is unfortunate, and perhaps even dangerous. It is hoped that this volume will encourage further discussion.

James. W. Firnberg
William F. Lasher
Editors

James W. Firnberg is assistant vice-president for academic affairs and director of institutional research for the Louisiana State University system. He is also professor of educational research at Louisiana State University–Baton Rouge. He is a charter member and past president of the Association for Institutional Research.

William F. Lasher is associate vice-president for budget and institutional studies at The University of Texas at Austin. He has worked in the field of institutional research since 1970 and is the immediate past president of the Association for Institutional Research.

The effective communication of desired information between the human generator and the human user requires one to accommodate variances in decision-making style, behavior, and context.

The Pragmatic Imperative of Institutional Research

William L. Tetlow

The most common response to the question "What is institutional research?" is one that stresses those applied research activities undertaken in association with specific planning, policy, or decision situations. The stated objective is information, not just data, and the unstated premise is that decision making in organizations follows the classic rational model.

Saupe (1981) provides a conceptually richer exposition of the nature and purpose of institutional research, but nevertheless concludes by stating, "Institutional research has been described as an attitude of commitment to the value of the institution's purpose in society and to the value of critical appraisal and careful investigation. Institutional governance is *informed and rational* to the degree that such an attitude pervades the institutions" (p. 3). (Emphasis added.)

Information Utilization: Expectations Versus Reality

According to Feldman and March (1981), this assumption of rational decison making leads to some simplistic expectations for the utilization of information: "Relevant information will be gathered and analyzed prior to decision making. Information gathered for use in a decision will be used in making that decision. Available information will be examined before more information is gathered or requested. Needs for information will be determined prior to asking for information. Information that is not relevant to a decision will not be gathered" (p. 172).

However, the authors summarize the literature concerned with studies of the gathering and actual use of information in organizations and report six phenomena:

> 1. Much of the information that is gathered and communicated by individuals and organizations has little decision relevance.
> 2. Much of the information that is used to justify a decision is collected and interpreted after the decision has been made, or substantially made.
> 3. Much of the information gathered in response to requests for information is not considered in the making of decisions for which it was requested.
> 4. Regardless of the information available at the time a decision is first considered, more information is requested.
> 5. Complaints that an organization does not have enough information to make a decision occur while available information is ignored.
> 6. The relevance of the information provided in the decision-making process to the decision being made is less conspicuous than is the insistence on information.
>
> In short, most organizations and individuals often collect more information than they use or can reasonably expect to use in the making of decisions. At the same time, they appear to be constantly needing or requesting more information, or complaining about inadequacies in information [p. 174].

It would appear, then, that the classic rational model of decision making still represents an ideal to be attained, rather than the norm. Jones (1982, p. 27) states categorically that "no one has been able to isolate an instance of provably unadulterated rational decision making, either in higher education or in any other sector of our society." Veteran information specialists, a fraternity to which institutional researchers belong, would undoubtedly concur with Jones.

The typical response of institutional researchers is to concur with the observations, decry the situation, and proceed with the assumption that rationality will ultimately prevail. They fail to recognize that the core activity of information provision, and the core problem for information science, is to facilitate the effective communication of desired information between the human generator and the human user (Belkin, 1978).

Data, Information, and the Context of Decision Making

Information, not data, is the objective. Information consists of data that have been selected, organized, and analyzed, so that they convey to the recipient user some useful knowledge (Jones, 1982; Walker, 1981). The very process of selection and organization of data involves many human judgments on the part of the information specialist. People differ significantly over what constitutes information for them, but frequently those who design information systems or perform analyses do not adequately understand the perspective of the decision maker or the full context of the decision situation (Jones, 1982). Administrators must synthesize a plan of action from a world of people, values, preferences, aspirations, interpersonal dynamics, facts, resources, and constraints (Lawrence and Service, 1977).

Data and information "enter into all manner of partisan and adversary contexts" (Jones, 1982, p. 15). Baldridge (1971) argues that decision making is essentially a political art because decision processes are full of conflict. Interest groups articulate their interests in many different ways, bring pressure to bear on the decision-making process, and use power and force when available and necessary. This phenomenon of the politicization of the institutional research function appears to be the natural consequence of the proliferation of data in our society, prevailing social norms, and a belief in rational decision processes of a particular kind (Feldman and March, 1981).

Alternative norms and decision-making processes do exist, however, and institutional researchers should do more than give token acknowledgment to the alternatives. "It is not hard to imagine a society in which requests for information and insistence on reports and analyses would be signs of indecisiveness or lack of faith" (Feldman and March, 1981, p. 178).

Feldman and March cite four principal reasons why organizations request information and reports and frequently do not use them for decision making.

First, organizations provide incentives for gathering extra information because the cost and benefits of information are not all incurred at the same place in the organization. The decisions to gather information frequently are made in one division while the costs of data collection are incurred in others. Thus, there are incentives for extra data gathering since the requester frequently does not incur or is not cognizant of any cost implications. Furthermore, since post hoc accountability is often required, it is better from the decision maker's point of view to have information that is not needed rather than not having information that might be needed.

The second reason proposed is that organizations often gather information for the purpose of monitoring their environment, that is, in a surveillance mode, rather than in a decision mode. "Organizations scan the environment for surprises as much as they try to clarify uncertainties" (p. 182).

Third, they suggest that most information that is generated and processed in an organization is subject to strategic misrepresentation. Information is gathered and communicated in a context of conflict, with a consciousness of potential consequences that makes the innocence of information problematic. Frequently, information is produced in order to persuade someone to do something.

Fourth, decision making in organizations constitutes an arena for exercising social values, for displaying proper behavior with respect to intelligent and rational choice. Therefore, it is suggested that the gathering of information provides a ritualistic assurance that proper attitudes about decision making exist in the organization. "Using information, asking for information, and justifying decisions in terms of information have all come to be significant ways in which we symbolize that the process is legitimate, that we are good decision makers, and that our organizations are well managed" (Feldman and March, 1981, p. 178).

Sabatler (1978, p. 397) adds what could be considered a fifth reason for the apparent nonuse of information. He notes that "no policy decision can be based solely on technical information. Normative elements invariably enter, whether the value choices come from statute, the personal philosophies of administrative officials, or their efforts to balance the preferences of competing constituencies."

The Legacy of Rationality

If actual data and information usage and actual decision making are so much at odds with the classic rational model of decision making, how are we to understand the continued belief in the model on the part of many institutional researchers? In part, at least, the answer lies in the historical development of the profession.

The history of the institutional research function actually began several millenia ago under markedly different conditions in European and Asian institutions of higher learning. In North America, the assistance that the founders of Yale obtained from Harvard in 1701 has been cited by Cowley (1960) as the first piece of institutional research in American higher education.

However, colleges existing in the seventeenth and eighteenth centuries were not inclined to engage in critical self-examination. The purposes of higher education were reasonably clear and generally not challenged, and institutional research studies were not conducted on a systematic basis (Cowley, 1960).

It was not until the beginning of the twentieth century that the social norms of American society and a strong belief in the value of the scientific method supported the case for "systematic fact finding and research in the administration of higher education" (Scroggs, 1938). An entire era of surveys ensued which had a strong impact on higher education. Among the reasons cited for the surveys were the development of the scientific spirit in education, the "efficiency" and social survey movements, and the growth, complexity, and cost of higher education.

The extensive increases in institutional size and complexity that commenced after World War II led to the formalization of the institutional research function as college officials sought greater understanding and control of their institutions. The formalization process went hand in hand with the belief that the scientific method, proven to be so useful for discovering new knowledge, could be equally useful as the basis for good decision making. The operations research phenomenon, which developed out of experiences in World War II, embodied this belief for many of our major corporations, as well as for the Defense Department. The 1960s and 1970s witnessed the development and use in business and government of various planning and budgeting models (such as planning, programming, and budgeting systems and zero-based budgeting) that were explicitly grounded in assumptions of rationality. In short, the professionalization of institutional research occurred at a time when the belief in, and advocacy of, rational decision making was at its peak. It is not altogether surprising, then, that the rational model, with its explicitly normative perspective, still heavily influences our conduct of institutional research.

Alternative Views of Decision Making

Even at the zenith of the belief in the rational model of decision making, there were dissenters. At the present time, a number of views can claim at least a coterie of followers. Recently the literature on decision making has been classified into five main schools of thought (Keen and Morton, 1978, p. 62ff):

1. *The rational-manager view* — the classic conception based on the assumption of a rational, completely informed, single decision maker.
2. *The "satisficing" process-oriented view* — based on Simon's (1957) notion of "bounded rationality" with an emphasis on heuristic rules of thumb and a search for solutions that are "good enough."
3. *The organizational procedures view* — which stresses the importance of organizational roles, channels of communicating, and system relationships.
4. *The political view* — which entails a personalized bargaining process with outcomes determined by power and influence (Baldridge, 1971).
5. *The individual-differences perspective* — which concentrates on the individual manager's problem-solving behavior and is contingent upon his or her style, background and personality.

Keen and Morton conclude their review as follows: "There seems to be no self-evidently right way to look at the decision-making process. For a given situation, the 'correct' way may involve a blend of all five points of view, or the particular context may make one of them the most relevant. Because of the multidimensional nature of decision making, it is critical to *diagnose* which aspect(s) is the most pivotal in any situation" (p. 63).

The role of the institutional researcher — to provide information that supports institutional planning, policy formulation, and decision making — must therefore not be restricted to one decision-making school of thought or one notion of "rationality." Instead, institutional researchers should be prepared to adapt their activities to the decision context, the personality and style of the decision maker, and the intended use of the information they provide.

The Pragmatic Imperative

Thus, the pragmatic imperative for all engaged in providing information to decision makers in higher education—that is, institutional researchers by any title—is to:
- Understand that not all information that is requested will be used to influence a decision
- Diagnose the style and method used by the decision maker(s) and determine which dimensions are pivotal
- Recognize that one's concept of the decision-making process largely predetermines one's response to other people's logic, behavior, and opinions
- Take into account the situational context of the decision.

Reputations for effective institutional research are built upon capabilities for providing useful information in a timely and intelligent manner.

References

Baldridge, V. J. *Power and Conflict in the University: Research in the Sociology of Complex Organizations.* New York: Wiley, 1971.

Belkin, N. J. "Information Concepts for Information Science." *Journal of Documentation,* 1978, *34,* 55-85.

Cowley, W. H. "Two and a Half Centuries of Institutional Research." In R. Axt and T. S. Hall (Eds.), *College Self-Study: Lectures on Institutional Research.* Boulder, Colo.: Western Interstate Commission for Higher Education, 1960.

Feldman, M. S., and March, J. G. "Information in Organizations as Signal and Symbol." *Administrative Science Quarterly,* 1981, *26,* 171-186.

Jones, D. P. *Data and Information for Executive Decisions in Higher Education.* Boulder, Colo.: National Center for Higher Education Management Systems, 1982.

Keen, P. G. W., and Morton, M. S. S. *Decision Support Systems: An Organizational Perspective.* Reading, Mass.: Addison-Wesley, 1978.

Lawrence, G. B., and Service, A. L. *Quantitative Approaches in Higher Education Management: Potential, Limits, and Challenge.* Washington, D.C.: American Association for Higher Education, 1977.

Sabatler, P. "The Acquisition and Utilization of Technical Information by Administrative Agencies." *Administrative Science Quarterly,* 1978, *23,* 396-417.

Saupe, J. L. *The Functions of Institutional Research.* Tallahassee, Fla.: The Association for Institutional Research, 1981.

Scroggs, S. *Systematic Fact Finding and Research in the Administration of Higher Education.* Ann Arbor, Mich.: Edwards, 1938.

Simon, H. A. *Administrative Behavior.* New York: Macmillan, 1957.

Walker, D. E. "The Organization and Use of Information: Contributions of Information Science, Computational Linguistics and Artificial Intelligence." *Journal of the American Society for Information Science,* September 1981, 347-363.

William L. Tetlow is the director of the Information for Management Program at the National Center for Higher Education Management Systems. He is a past president of the Association for Institutional Research and prior to his present position served for eighteen years as a faculty member and institutional research director.

The politics of information on most college and university campuses may be readily seen in national, regional, and statewide concern with planning, management, and evaluation.

The Politics of Information

Cameron L. Fincher

The political implications of information undoubtedly began with primitive people's belief in sympathetic magic. Possession of another's personal property was believed to give great power over that person, and possession of an enemy's name presumably gave strategical and tactical advantages. Vestiges of sympathetic magic may be evident in contemporary use of first names for answering the phone, signing letters, and introducing ourselves at cocktail parties.

In academe, vestiges of sympathetic magic may be found in the eagerness with which we seek knowledge of another person's salary, assigned duties, and departmental budget. Many of us are curious about the amount of lucrativeness of our colleagues' consulting and their demand as after-dinner speakers. "To know someone" or to be "in the know" still has colloquial implications of power or advantage.

Higher education is often identified as a knowledge industry, and knowledge is believed by many to be the basis of the postindustrial or postmodern society in which we live. Information-processing models give good insight into the workings of the human mind, and few topics have consumed as much time or outside funding in the last twenty years as management information systems. Federal, state, and local government agencies display an insatiable appetite for information, and no feature of organizational or institutional management is more demanding than its information-processing chores. It is not fanciful to speak and write, as many have done, of our informational society.

The availability, distribution, and uses of information are often the roots of conflict between academic administrators and faculty, central authority and institutional autonomy, professional staff and governing board, and public officials and institutional leaders. The recording and reporting functions in higher education, once thought to be the delegated responsibility of registrars, are believed by many to vitiate faculty creativity, stultify administrative leadership, impede institutional development, and overwhelm governing or coordinating boards. The flow of information is usually seen as one-way, with facts and figures moving upward and outward, and with few pretenses of feedback, the best-known concept of information theory.

The collection and derivation of information thus begins in political circumstance, and politics may always be the other side of the informational coin. It is difficult to imagine a recorded fact or figure for which some unanticipated and unintended political use might not be found. And on alternate occasions institutions of higher education have been politically damned for *not* recording and reporting information they were previously damned *for* recording and reporting. If knowledge is power, and humans are political animals, the politics of information is undoubtedly what institutional research and management in the 1980s are all about.

Definition of Terms

Data and Information. The meaning of information in institutional research and management is aided by distinctions that should be made between data and information at one level, and between information and knowledge at another. Data are best identified as the specific facts and details that are recorded in the routine operation of institutions. The recruitment, selection, and enrollment of students, for example, now require massive amounts of data. High school records and standardized test scores are but the tip of the data iceberg as applying students seek financial aid, entrance to programs of high demand, participation in campus life, and genuine academic advising or counseling. The facts reported on innumerable forms by individual students do not become information until they are organized and distilled for specific institutional decisions and individual choices.

Data-processing technology has resulted in several generations of college students who answer questions not by speaking or writing but by filling in the space enclosed by parallel lines or circles. More often than not, the data supplied by students must be entered in predetermined categories for data-processing purposes. Much too often the data thus supplied by students were more easily aggregated than analyzed and interpreted. Summaries of data were used by administrative officials such as registrars and deans for decisions of sectioning and placing, but appreciable advancement in data-processing technology was necessary before the data could be reported in usable form back to the students or onward to other administrators.

Advances in computer technology have made possible what data-processing equipment could not. Student data can now be organized and analyzed for multiple purposes and uses. Specific facts and figures can be reclassified and high-speed printers make possible a wealth of information for other clientele and users. Data become information when they are organized, analyzed, and interpreted for use. Data can be, and often are, collected and stored without retrieval and use that give them informational value. Data become information as they are retrieved because of the remarkable blending of retrieving and analyzing. In brief, students' grades and scores can be retrieved as means, standard deviations, and correlation coefficients and not merely as individual transcripts or frequency counts.

Until they are retrieved and used in some kind of analyzable or interpretable form, data are no doubt apolitical. Yet the fear of retrieval and use of data for political purposes has been a major criticism of data banks that apparently accumulate massive detail without adequate guarantees of protection to individuals and their rights to privacy. Data thus have a potential, if not actual, political implication that critics of an informational society believe to be Orwellian.

Information is perhaps always political in its implications. Organization, analysis, and interpretation must be for some purpose, but once data become information through organization and analysis, the information is subject to more than one interpretation. Student grades are indicative of data that are collected and stored for fairly specific purposes, but they are seldom analyzed and reported on any basis other than the individual's transcript, for fear of the many, and presumably erroneous, interpretations that can be made. There is a distinct possibility that, given a choice, many college instructors would have their bank accounts published instead of their grade distributions.

Institutions of higher education obviously have need for data other than those collected in daily, routine operations. Research data are the prime example of detailed facts that are recorded for specific purposes of analysis and interpretation. Informed consent, as a requirement of research involving human subjects, is indicative of the political sensitivities to which ostensibly objective, impartial data collection must be tuned. The use of human subjects in research now places political constraints on researchers because of potential abuse that might occur in the course of data gathering and because of the potential misuse that might be made of the research at a later time.

Institutional researchers have shown, on occasion, a preference for data processing, as opposed to information processing. Because of the political/legal/administrative implications of institutional data, some institutional researchers abstain with considerable skill from analyzing and interpreting the data they provide for administrative decisions and institutional management. In some cases, that is exactly what administrators insist that institutional researchers do. In other cases, it is merely a will to survive in political climates where heads often roll and institutional researchers prefer that it be someone else's head.

Information and Knowledge. If knowledge can be defined as the organization of information at higher levels of interpretation and explanation, knowledge may be less political than information because it is more public. At the same time, knowledge may be more political because its influence is more substantive and enduring. Notions of knowledge as higher levels of organized information suggest that the publicity given the "knowledge explosion" in contemporary society would have been more aptly described as an explosion of information. Virtually everyone is aware that information is available in quantities and with a rapidity unknown in other societies and at other stages of history. But while many speakers and writers marvel at the instant information obtainable with computer and communications technology, they are more reluctant to speak and write of instant knowledge. Cynics are not the only ones who believe that the massive information available to postmodern man has produced something less than massive, universal knowledge.

Knowledge is more often regarded as a public good than information is, and knowledge is more likely to be seen as belonging in the public domain. The public's right to be informed is frequently acknowledged, but so is the public's right to know. In much the same manner, copyrights are granted authors of books, but such pertains to the specific wording of the information given and not to the knowledge readers can gain from purchasing and reading the book. Other writers are not supposed to use the book without due permission and citation. But if the book provides useful knowledge, readers are given great freedom in the uses they make of the knowledge.

The point of transition at which information becomes knowledge is more difficult to define than the point at which data become information. The analysis and interpretation of data are appreciative occurrences, almost like the preparation of a meal. The uses of knowledge in administrative decisions and problem solving, however, may be too subtle for many institutional researchers to appreciate. If administrators were better cooks, they could prepare their own meals but it would be a faulty division of institutional labor. Thus, institutional researchers who supply data or information for administrative decision making and institutional management should gain substantial knowledge in the process.

The Political Pressures for Information

Institutional research, management information, and institutional planning and development are the products of political pressures brought to bear upon institutions of higher education in an unprecedented period of growth and expansion. As colleges and universities became more dependent upon federal funding, there was an increased demand for uniform reporting systems that federal agencies could use in their documentation of societal demands and expectations for education beyond high school. As higher education within the separate states became centralized with statewide governing and coordinating boards, state agencies placed a heavier burden upon institutions for enrollment, financial, and facilities data. As the public became suspicious that all was not well in the nation's efforts to provide mass education at the college level, private foundations, public commissions, and national councils accelerated their plea that institutions become more rational and analytical in their planning, management, and development.

Internal political pressures were present in the increasing organizational complexity of colleges and universities as they recruited faculty and expanded campus facilities to meet increased enrollments. Numbers alone might account for the student protests that began in 1964 but much can be explained by cultural pluralism and the astounding variation in student preparation and motivation. To meet classes of underestimated size, faculty were recruited from newly established graduate programs, the ministry, the military services, and other sources where academic traditions and values may not have been evident. To meet the different demands and expectations of their pluralistic clientele, institutions often diversified their programs and courses of instruction without having well-qualified teaching faculty, instructional resources, or institutional commitments.

Federal funding policies and practices, in reflexive efforts to meet societal demands, have vacillated between the carrot and the stick. Legislative enactments of massive programs for the relief of societal ills were too often the carrot that could not match the stick of federal court rulings and federal agency guidelines. Yet, given the confusion of sticks and carrots, the response of institutions of higher education will be recalled as admirable, and it may well be evaluated in later years as more successful than anyone had a right to expect.

The politicization of American colleges and universities, nonetheless, was a shock from which institutions did not recover quickly. Yet, notable success can be seen in the professional specialty of institutional research itself, an impressive array of planning concepts and techniques, a more mature cadre of academic administrators, and a diversification of educational functions and services that may be regarded as healthy and wholesome in a society much given to democratic ideals. Perhaps the most impressive accomplishment, however, is the flow of information that is now available to institutions of higher education.

A National Center for Education Statistics (NCES) now publishes data on institutional enrollments, finances, facilities, resources, and results that give valuable and useful information about the national commitment to postsecondary education. An Educational Resources Information Center (ERIC) releases periodic summaries or guides to the research on topical issues that approach interpretation and provides access through microfiche or hard photocopy to most of the educational research done in the nation's 3,000 institutions of postsecondary education. Factbooks are published and widely distributed by national associations, regional agencies, state commissions, and various institutions.

The flow of such massive amounts of data is an undeniable function of political forces, and the widespread distribution of enrollment and financial data is often an acknowledged tactic to depoliticize institutional relations by taking the stance that the institution has nothing to hide. The uses and applications of so much data and information, however, remain uncertain or difficult to determine. Institutional planning, management, and development are obviously dependent upon information about institutional missions, goals, faculties, programs, students, facilities, and finances. But the uses of such information vary with administrative style, notions of accountability, and other situational or institutionally specific factors. The extent to which administrative decisons are based on data or information is particularly difficult to determine. The extent to which institutional policies are based on hard facts and figures is similarly obscure.

The Political Uses of Information

At the national level Caplan, Morrison, and Stambaugh (1975) present evidence that policy makers are receptive to information gained through research in the social sciences. Demographic data and economic trend data are regarded as the most valid social science information, however, and appreciable evidence was gathered that policy makers may differ in their information-processing styles. The three styles identified in the study were clinical, academic, and advocacy, but at least 30 percent of the survey respondents exhibited a mixed style. Perhaps significant is the finding that policy makers with an advocacy style of information processing made the least use of social science information. When such information is used with officials with an advocacy style, the information is used in an "extrascientific" manner with skillful ignorance of valid information that does not fit into the prevailing political climate.

Lindblom and Cohen (1979) are dubious of the uses that policy makers and problem solvers make of information gained from the social sciences. Research on the uses of research information tends to center exclusively on contemporary studies to the ignorance of the large issues involved and the larger body of research literature that exists in many policy-related fields. Lindblom and Cohen thus contend that in both government policy making and social problem solving, the suppliers of information are disappointed because they are not heard and the users are disenchanted because they obtain so little that is relevant to the issue.

The uses of research-based information in the formulation of public policy remains a mystery for many institutional researchers. Information given in the form of testimony at congressional hearings is apparently influential in the initial stages of legislative enactment, but the direct or immediate impact of that information is difficult to trace in final versions of legislative acts. The misuse of information or its conspicuous absence may be easier to appreciate.

At the institutional level the political uses of information would also appear to be a function of the information-processing styles of institutional leaders. Clinical, academic, and advocacy styles might be much in evidence in carefully conducted studies. Wilensky (1969) has identified three roles or functions in organizational intelligence that are observable on many college campuses. Both presidents and institutional researchers are sometimes seen as contact people, internal communications specialists, or facts-and-figures people. Institutional information must be shared in appropriate ways with outside governmental agencies, community leaders, and the various clientele served by the institution. In a similar manner, institutional information must be disseminated among faculty, students, and campus agencies. Administrators suspected of withholding information that should be shared with others will inevitably wind up in political difficulty.

Institutional factbooks have been an effective means in many institutions of politically defusing administration–faculty relations, shoring up administration–student relations, and creating in other respects an atmosphere of informational give and take. Enrollment figures, faculty workloads, and institutional expenditures are disclosed to all who care to make use of such information. The publication of average faculty salaries by rank apparently dispels some of the secrecy with which faculty salaries have often been enshrouded. State legislators would no doubt like to see more information about institutions' auxiliary enterprises, but by and large, the publication of institutional factbooks has been a telling feature of the information revolution in higher education.

Technological advances in microcomputers, word processors, and telecommunications bid well to alter administrative styles in many significant ways. The presence of microcomputers at the departmental level means that much useful information can be generated at whichever administrative level it is needed. The availability of word processors should mean a lessening of the tension that comes from unwanted record-keeping functions and an ease of communication with other campus agencies. Telecommunications may succeed in making statewide systems of higher education and multicampus institutions what they were presumed to be in the 1960s, and efficient means of effecting economies of scale.

The political implications of microcomputers, word processors, and telecommunications should move the politics of information into a more mature stage of interinstitutional cooperation and institutional effectiveness. The politics of higher education is apparently intensified by the absence or suppression of information more than by easy and ready access. Many political questions remain, nonetheless, in the form of collection, distribution, and use. Centralized record-keeping functions should be greatly supplemented by departmental or program information-processing capabilities, but questions of which data are to be used by whom for what purposes must be answered satisfactorily.

The Politics of Planning, Management, and Evaluation

The availability of massive data and copious information includes no guarantees that the data and information will be useful or that they will be used. Those who supply and distribute information on national, regional, and state levels cannot always anticipate the informational needs and interests of users, and by the time much information is available to users, the need for its use has passed. The penchant for crisis management in higher education suggests that academic administrators and researchers have an abiding faith in information and its relevance to the solution of institutional problems. Crises invariably produce a frantic search for data or information that will have an ameliorative effect. Most crises close with resolution, no doubt, that next time everyone will be better prepared and the information will be available.

In some crises, the information needed or desired may have been available but its relevance was not recognized. The supplier's method of classifying, aggregating, and reporting data may have obscured their applicability to the situation. The information-processing styles of administrators and researchers may thus be more of an occupational hazard than previously recognized. Institutional leaders are known to have categorical preferences, and information in the other person's categories may not be information that is usable. The Census Bureau evidently has had years of experience trying to satisfy the categorical preferences of users—and failing to do so. Categories that appear highly serviceable at the time data are collected are sometimes nonfunctional by the time the data are reported.

The federal government's efforts to establish uniform data-reporting systems for 3,000 postsecondary institutions has been less than successful. The program categories of the Higher Education General Information Survey (HEGIS), for example, have been subtly and sometimes "creatively" distorted by faculty, campus reporters, and institutional officials. Both institutional leaders and governing boards have been surprised to learn from HEGIS reports that their institutions were offering academic programs of which no one was aware. In other instances, institutions have been amazed at the generosity or paucity of

FTE allotments by state legislatures to the students within the institution.

A telling point might be that categories for data collection, analysis, and reporting are like computer programs and must be subject to continuing, if not compulsive, tinkering. Much the same might be said about federal policies and funding for more effective planning, management, and evaluation in institutions of higher education. Generous funding of the National Center for Higher Education Management Systems (NCHEMS) has resulted in an impressive array of tools and techniques that should be applicable to the problems of planning, management, and evaluation. The extent to which these tools and techniques have been adopted by institutions of higher education, however, is a matter about which better information is needed. The extent to which institutional planning, management, and evaluation have been improved through the application of systematic concepts and techniques is a matter about which little information is available. Such information as policy makers might have suggests that NCHEMS products have been well publicized and favorably received in many institutions, but there should be better evidence of the effectiveness of such concepts and techniques in improving institutional management and effectiveness.

The Politics of Planning. National planning in higher education remains a subject about which there is great ambivalence and for which national goals or purposes remain quite vague and confused. Funding policies and priorities are subject to the changing policies and priorities of administrations that change suddenly and drastically. Despite the massive programs of aid to institutions and students, the creation of such agencies as the National Institute of Education and the Fund for the Improvement of Postsecondary Education and the ambitious efforts of regional labs and research and development centers, national purpose and federal policies in higher education do not establish a climate or environment in which comprehensive planning is possible.

Regional goals and priorities conducive to planning have been much more in evidence. The Southern Regional Education Board (SREB) has been particularly successful in defining regional goals and objectives for higher education in the South, identifying priorities for state and institutional action, and providing, through periodic factbooks, data and information that are useful for planning purposes. The success of SREB in serving the southern region was instrumental in the establishment of the Education Commission of the States (ECS) and its apparent desire to serve as a counterbalance in the federal-state relations that influence the development of education.

Federal policies have encouraged statewide planning efforts through the 1202 Commissions funded under the Educational Amendments Act of 1972. California, for example, has been able to develop an information digest which displays, for the first time, the scope and complexity of postsecondary education in a state where at least 10 percent of the nation's college students are enrolled (California Postsecondary Education Commission, 1981). Georgia, as another example, has been able to define statewide goals and objectives for postsecondary agencies and institutions within the state. When funds from the federal government succumbed to Reaganomics, the state of Georgia assumed the costs of conducting a statewide assessment of postsecondary goals and objectives (Governor's Committee on Postsecondary Education, 1980).

The encouragement of institutional planning has been significantly influenced by federal, regional, and state policies. National, regional, and state trends can be gleaned from NCES documents and other government publications with planning implications. Good assistance may be obtained from the efforts of the federal government to fund the development of instruments for the definition of institutional missions, goals, and outcomes. Efforts to foster program planning and development have been less direct but noticeably successful in selected institutions (Andersen, 1980; Dearman and Plisko, 1981; Fincher, 1979; Frankel and Gerald, 1980; Grant and Eiden, 1981).

The Politics of Management. Judging from the amount of funding and attendant coverage in the professional literature, the development of management information systems (MIS) has been a noticeably high priority of federal and state government. Also promoted, but with a varying emphasis, has been the adoption of specific management techniques such as planning, programming, budgeting systems (PPBS), management by objectives (MBO), and zero based budgeting (ZBB). The political pressures for management systems and techniques stem from the charges of mismanagement filed against institutions of higher education in the wake of student protest and faculty dissent. The national enchantment with total MIS was short-lived and soon was replaced with computer planning models in which MIS was an inherent feature.

The motives for management systems and techniques can be seen in retrospect as entirely political. The forms of information generated by MIS were seldom usable by or useful to those responsible for institutional and program management. Without exception, MIS supplied information of interest to centralized authority in the form of statewide governing boards, state planning and budgeting offices, and federal regulatory agencies. Data were reported in forms acceptable to external persons and agencies who were under pressure to demonstrate public accountability for the federal, state, and foundation funds lavished upon institutions of higher education in its period of growth and expansion. The message so clearly conveyed by critics and observers was to the effect that colleges and universities had been derelict in managing their internal affairs and emulation of the nation's business corporations was the only feasible solution.

The response to political pressures for MIS, PPBS, MBO, and ZBB was itself political. Some institutional leaders adopted a tactic of, "If you can't beat them, join them," while others adopted tactics of overkill. The outcome is obviously a more "public accounting" of institutional affairs and an abundance of management information for external consumption. The extent to which MIS, PPBS, MBO, and ZBB—as advocated and supposedly adopted—changed administrative information-processing styles and institutional operations and practices is a question deserving further study. It can be observed, nonetheless, that scientists, humanists, and professionals of remarkable diversity continued to be appointed presidents or chancellors, and that no research has ever suggested that any particular academic discipline or professional specialty equips its novitiates uncommonly well for institutional leadership.

The Politics of Evaluation. If the demands for planning and management information can be absolved of outright politics in their origin, the same is not true of the demand for evaluation. Critics both within higher education and without were dissatisfied with the state of internal affairs in academe and with their results. The concern for outcomes can still be dated, without distortion, from the Coleman report of 1966. If education at all levels had been exclusively concerned with inputs and processes prior to that time, no such claims can be made for the years following.

The evaluations supposedly mandated in the federal legislation of the mid 1960s might have been pro forma riders or attachments in a political climate different from that of the late 1960s and early 1970s. There is no denying, however, that evaluation of federally funded projects did become obligatory, and accountability did become something other than a fiscal accounting of expenditures for funded projects and programs. The rapid emergence of evaluation specialists did not lessen the shock to many institutions that were required, for the first time, to account for contracts and grants in terms of results, as well as expenditures.

Information about results, however, required specific and concrete information about project and program objectives. Whereas goals and objectives may have been superficially assumed or casually inferred in climates less concerned with regulation, proposal writers in the 1970s often found that the most difficult parts of their proposals dealt with objectives that were observable, quantifiable, and obtainable. Project and programs directors were sometimes required for the first time in their professional experience to say what they were going to do, how they were going to do it, and what results they would achieve in doing so. Moreover, they were often required to demonstrate institutional commitments to societal objectives not easily accomplished in funded projects supposedly educational in nature.

One dimension of the political pressures for evaluation must be recognized as punitive. Funding agency personnel, if not the agency itself, sometimes took an uncompromising stance that funded institutions were guilty of societal wrongdoing, institutional ineptness, or crass deficiencies of institutional character. It was not unheard of for a proposal to be funded with moralistic overtones serving notice that the funded project and its personnel were on probation for the duration of the grant. The extent to which institutions were on the defensive and the moral indignation with which funds could be granted in the 1970s is a researchable topic worthy of its own funding.

In brief, the politics of evaluation have produced an extensive library of evaluation concepts, methods, techniques, outcomes, and critiques. Much of this information remains in the files of funding agencies or in the form of interim reports that may never be completed. At some later time, however, the primary outcome of the politics of evaluation may be that it, too, has produced a different information-processing style for institutions of higher education (Fincher, 1981).

Summary and Conclusions

The politics of information has been discussed in this chapter as a necessity of institutional life. The records-keeping and data-reporting functions of colleges and universities have political implications that are both subtle and profound. Many of these political implications are difficult to anticipate because of the legal/political/administrative climate in which colleges and universities found themselves in the late 1960s and early 1970s. The political pressures upon institutions of higher education have no doubt produced different administrative styles that can be characterized as information-processing styles. Many important features of American institutions are "information-driven," and remarkable advances in computer and communications technology imply that ours is indeed an informational society.

The increasing scope and complexity of higher education in an information society lend substance to the inherent political power of information. The political uses of information are numerous, sometimes subtle, and sometimes brutal. The politics of information on most college and university campuses may be readily seen in national, regional, and statewide concern with planning, management, and evaluation. Concepts, methods, and information-processing styles in each of these three institutional functions have been greatly influenced by political pressures in the past fifteen years, and each is regarded as a proper concern of public policy in the 1980s.

References

Andersen, C. J. *1980 Factbook for Academic Administrators.* Washington, D.C.: American Council on Education, 1980.

California Postsecondary Education Commission. *Postsecondary Education in California: 1981 Information Digest.* Sacramento: California Postsecondary Education Commission, 1981.

Caplan, N., Morrison, A., and Stambaugh, R. J. *The Use of Social Science Knowledge in Policy Decisions at the National Level.* Ann Arbor: Institute for Social Research, University of Michigan, 1975.

Dearman, N. B., and Plisko, V. W. *The Condition of Education: 1981 Edition.* Washington, D.C.: National Center for Education Statistics, 1981.

Fincher, C. L. "The Packaging of Planning." *Research in Higher Education,* 1979, *11,* 365-368.

Fincher, C. L. "Literature of Program Evaluation." *Research in Higher Education,* 1981, *14,* 277-280.

Frankel, M. M., and Gerald, D. E. *Projections of Education Statistics to 1988-89.* Washington, D.C.: National Center for Education Statistics, 1980.

Governor's Committee on Postsecondary Education. *Georgia Postsecondary Education in the Eighties: Goals and Objectives.* Atlanta, Ga.: Governor's Committee on Postsecondary Education, 1980.

Grant, W. V., and Eiden, L. J. *Digest of Education Statistics 1981.* Washington, D.C.: National Center for Education Statistics, 1981.

Lindblom, C., and Cohen, D. K. *Usable Knowledge: Social Science and Social Problem Solving.* New Haven, Conn.: Yale University Press, 1979.

Wilensky, H. L. *Organizational Intelligence: Knowledge and Policy in Government and Industry.* New York: Basic Books, 1969.

Cameron L. Fincher is Regents Professor of higher education and psychology and director of the Institute of Higher Education at the University of Georgia. He is a charter member of the Association for Institutional Research and has received the association's Outstanding Service Award.

This chapter suggests ways that institutional researchers can analyze the political nature of their institutions and better understand the role institutional research plays in that environment.

Politics Within the Institution

Laura E. Saunders

Institutional researchers have traditionally not paid much attention to how their studies are received or the ultimate effect they have on the institution. Institutional research literature concentrates on the descriptions of how to conduct institutional research studies, methodologies for analysis of data and refined techniques for estimating and projection. Many institutional researchers operate as if they exist in a rational world where decisions are arrived at logically on the basis of information and data. As a result many studies are relegated to the shelf, and never used for decisions.

The researcher needs to understand the political setting in order to insure that institutional research is influential and becomes the basis for action. This chapter suggests some ways that institutional researchers can analyze the political nature of their institutions and better understand the role institutional research plays in that environment.

Elements of a Political University

A recent ERIC publication defines politics within higher education as "concerned basically with patterns of interaction or conflict over values, interests, and goals, relating to the perceived needs of higher education" (Hines, 1980, p. 3). Politics as used in this discussion includes the study and analysis of power, influence, and authority as they are manifested within an institution, particularly with respect to establishing policy.

Analysis of the politics of universities has been based on studying interest groups, interaction and conflict patterns, bargaining and negotiation patterns, and the influence of particular groups within institutions. Political models of universities predict outcomes different from those typically given by bureaucratic, collegial, or rational models. In a political model, outcomes are seen as a result of a conflict process in which various groups press for particular objectives.

The institutional researcher may wish to pursue the politics of academic institutions by consulting recent works in this area. J. Victor Baldridge provides an overview of the literature of politics in *Policy Making and Effective Leadership* (1978). A brief analytical framework for reviewing political aspects of an organization is given by Baldridge in *Power and Conflict in the University* (1971) and includes as elements for study:

- The social context—the interest groups existing in an institution
- Articulation—how the interest groups exert pressure and influence policy
- Transformation—how the pressures are translated into policy
- Implementation and execution—how the policy is put into effect and the actual effectiveness of the policy on the institution.

The more recent work by Baldridge (1978) amplifies and extends this model, applying it to a cross section of institutions. Discussions of particular interest groups within a university also can be found in Talcott Parsons, *The American University;* Christopher Jencks and David Riesman, *The Academic Revolution;* John Millett, *The Academic Community;* and Frederick E. Balderston, *Managing Today's University.*

After studying the interest groups and political processes within an institution, institutional researchers need to answer the question: How do they fit into the political process? To answer that question we need to review the traditional role performed by institutional research offices.

Role of Institutional Research

Paul Dressel (1979), one of the earliest spokesmen for institutional research, sees the traditional institutional researcher as "an individual who is interested in teaching and learning and who views institutional research as a way to identify, analyze, and study some of the major issues confronting higher education" (p. 48). Further, Dressel indicates: "For my own part, I have always believed—and still do—that institutional researchers should not become involved in making or carrying out decisions, that they should always distinguish between their own values and preferences and the logical import of data they analyze and that they should not expect that their studies will always be lauded and immediately acted upon" (p. 44). The elements of the traditional role herein described are clear: independence, scholarly analysis, and advisory status. This description is extended by other writers who suggest how the researcher should fulfill the role of providing independent analysis (Saupe and Montgomery, 1970). In order to utilize institutional research, (1) the function and value of institutional research must be understood by the faculty, (2) the principal spokesman for institutional research should be an accepted member of the administration and be trusted by the faculty, (3) cooperative working relations with other offices must be maintained, (4) current problems and issues must be known to the institutional research office, and (5) problems or issues must be anticipated before they occur.

These idealized descriptions of how the institutional researcher should function contrast with many experiences common to institutional researchers in which carefully prepared studies are set aside and decisions are based on forces and pressures only dimly comprehended. This traditional view of institutional research includes no role for the analyst in seeing that the conclusions or recommendations are actually adopted or are effective if they are adopted. Thus the institutional research office appears tangential to the main processes of the institution, engaged in producing reports that seldom are read or utilized.

The relevant issue here is the effectiveness of an institutional research office. Effectiveness can be construed in two regards: (1) with respect to the rationality of the process by which the decisions are arrived at, or (2) with respect to the likelihood that a particular judgment will prevail. The first deals with the substance of the work of institutional research while the second deals with whether or not anyone pays attention to the work. Institutional researchers have largely focused on the first aspect of effectiveness but have often ignored the second. Recently several writers have proposed ways of increasing effectiveness in the second sense—increasing the likelihood that the researcher's judgment will prevail.

Action research (Buhl and Lindquist, 1981) is defined as research that gets used. Action research proposes that research be tailored to provide for individuals a sound knowledge base upon which to decide whether or not to change. Action research makes the researcher a participant in the process by having him provide answers to questions about what is to be accomplished, how it is being done, what is stopping the process, and how the obstacles can be reduced. The writings on the *professional as change agent* also suggest a more active role (Haas, 1980). Haas notes that dramatically different patterns of behavior have lower probability of acceptance than recommendations that involve modifications to existing processes. He argues that the probability of adoption of a policy is increased if those who have to implement it are involved in the development of the policy. In addition, change processes must also provide assistance outside the immediate decision sphere to become part of the ongoing organization. Finally, Haas urges that strategies that can be adjusted to changing circumstances and actors are more likely to be adopted than rigid doctrines.

These recommendations for giving analysts a more active role only partially address the problem of effectiveness, for they do not fully treat the political nature of the institution. The analysis of political power, interest groups, conflict, and change supplies the missing ingredient in determining how to increase the likelihood that the researcher's view will prevail. The institutional researcher's objective is institutional influence. Most professional writing deals with another important objective, that of professional status as an institutional researcher, but for this paper institutional influence is the objective.

One interesting exception to the traditionally aloof research role for institutional research has been the gradual evolution of some offices into planning, resource allocation, and budget support offices. These offices take on a major internal role, but they are no longer doing traditional institutional research. Instead they are closely involved in assisting decision makers by providing information and analysis geared to day-to-day management problems. From being on the outside producing shelf documents, these offices have become vital parts of the management/decision process of a college or university.

How can the traditional office become more involved and effective, and hence better support the institution? Are there ways of reviewing the function of institutional research offices that will lead to a plan for becoming more effective? Applying a strategic planning analysis of the interface between the institution environment and the institutional research office suggests a way of developing such a plan.

Strategic Planning for the Institutional Research Function

Environmental Scan. An environmental scan consists of four steps: determining (1) the style of administration, (2) the functions the office performs, (3) the relevant formal and informal decision structures, and (4) the key actors. Identifying a metaphor describing the institution's governance or administrative style is a key to an accurate view of the institution and is needed to set the context for the detailed analysis of interest groups. Substantial variety in organizational styles exists within the administration of colleges and universities and different styles may apply to different decision makers. The dominant style will depend on the particular institutional framework, the historical development of the institution, external conditions, and leadership, as well as whether it is two- or four-year, and public or private. Cohen and March in their excellent book *Leadership and Ambiguity: The American College President* (1974) identify eight metaphors for institutions which serve as a useful shorthand for characterizing administrative style:

1. Competitive market—the university is a collection of offerings, students select what they want to take, faculty are entrepreneurs, and the movement of students and funding define who survives and who does not.

2. Administrative—the university is a bureaucracy with a well defined objective and organized structures, hierarchies, and tasks.

3. Collective bargaining—the university is made up of conflicting, competing groups, who bargain with each other for desired outcomes and then abide by a "contract."

4. Democracy—the university operates through elected representatives chosen by all affected participants.

5. Consensus—it is the traditional collegial model, in which decisions are arrived at through consensus.

6. Anarchy—each individual makes his or her own decisions without reference to overall goals.

7. Independent judiciary—an independent judge resolves issues and is selected by a process unrelated to the group being governed.

8. Plebiscitary autocracy—the university is governed by an independent autocrat whose position is reinforced by a plebiscite from time to time.

An accurate assessment of the prevalent style or styles in your institution is a basic step for the environmental scan, as the type and kind of institutional research function will be radically different under different administrative styles. Much of the basic "how to do institutional research" literature reflects the assumption that there is only one administrative style, and it is either rational bureaucratic or rational collegial style.

To illustrate the difficulties each of these potential administrative styles poses for the institutional research role, consider the role of the institutional research office in a highly bureaucratic administration, dominated by rules, policies, and procedures. In such an institution a research office concentrates on the production of routine reports, the careful elaboration of information on institutional operation, and the gathering and distribution of statistics. In an institution in which the prevalent style is closer to an organized anarchy, the institutional research office may find that careful, neat analyses and distribution of statistics leave the office widely perceived as ineffectual and outside the mainstream of institutional decision making. A free-ranging style that attempts to identify problems and match them up with solutions and influence the process may be more productive in an anarchy than the more rigidly constrained, traditional bureaucratic reporting. Misjudging institutional style in this case can have far-reaching consequences.

To identify the prevalent style or styles accurately is not an easy task, for there may well be a difference between the formal way things are done and the actual operation. A lengthy formal decision process may suggest the administrative model, but if the actual choice is made by a small group of faculty who dominate the senate, and then given to the president for ratification, another model may in fact be operant. The analyst may find it useful to describe the metaphors to a number of knowledgeable people on campus and gather their views about the dominant model, if one choice is not obvious. Specifying the kind of decision—whether it concerns a salary, a program change, or a budget level—may also help, as different metaphors may exist for different kinds of decisions.

To expand upon Cohen and March's analysis, Table 1 pairs institutional styles and appropriate role strategies for institutional researchers.

The environmental scan must also include an analysis of the historical role of the institutional research office. Most institutional researchers are not attempting to establish a new office but rather are continuing an established function in an established office. It is useful to review, as part of the environmental scan, how the office is perceived on the campus and the nature and kind of work that it has been produc-

Table 1. Institutional Styles and Appropriate Role Strategies for Institutional Researchers

Institutional Style	Institutional Research Role
Competitive Market	Records changes in student interest, forecasts changes in support and student interest, and draws attention to imbalances between resources and activity. Provides "market analysis" and may also suggest areas not presently offered that could attract students.
Administrative	Prepares routine reports and analyses based on operational data; reports on performance of units in meeting institutional objectives and goals. May serve as a monitor of institutional policies.
Collective Bargaining	Defines interest groups, supplies background information to interest groups, and assesses implications of outcomes arrived at by bargaining for other university functions.
Democracy	Provides available information to all parties; plays role of informing the electorate. May participate as one of the constituency.
Consensus	Provides information that becomes part of the process of arriving at decisions, may record progress toward consensus, and brings problems forward for consideration.
Anarchy	Operates as catalyst, tries to arrange linking of decisions and problems, and influences outcomes. Information-supplying role less important than in other models.
Independent Judiciary	Provides data and analysis to judge-leader in making decisions.
Plebiscitary Autocracy	Provides information to autocrat to use in making decisions; occasionally provides data to constituency to use when a plebiscite is held.

ing. Is the office a traditional research organization that analyzes student statistics, prepares research reports, and operates as an adjunct to an academic program? Is it involved in policy analysis, working closely with institutional decision makers? Perhaps it is an integral part of the budgetary and resource allocation policy process in which institutional research reports are closely tied to operational decisions. Determining the reaction to the historical role of the institutional research office is a part of the review. Reactions should be obtained not only from those to whom the office reports but from other campus groups as well.

The environmental scan must also include the identification of relevant decision structures and interest groups. Most institutional researchers work in an institutional environment characterized by more than one set of decision makers. Faculty pass on curriculum course offerings and the admission of students. Administrators allocate faculty positions. Faculty and administrators may jointly decide faculty salary increases while legislative bodies determine gross institutional budgets. In surveying the environment, relevant interest groups need to be identified with respect to a great variety of institutional activities and decisions. There may be an overall faculty body that advises the president or chief executive with respect to faculty views on broad policy issues. In addition, there may be particular faculty groups concerned with the administration of detailed decisions such as student admission standards or space assignment. Nonacademic staff often form an important interest group even if they do not always play a role in formal policy determination. Students constitute an important interest group, even if their views on issues may be hard to predict.

It is also important to keep in mind that the relevant interest groups for a particular decision will change and certainly will not be constant over time. As issues change and particularly in times of institutional stress, a given issue may serve as a "garbage can" to collect a variety of individuals. People may become participants in issues that are out of their ordinary purview simply because of the pressure of external events. Thus while participating groups can be identified with respect to past interest in issues, this does not always ensure that the same groups or persons will be the only people involved in similar issues in the future. The identification of new or emerging interest groups is also necessary. Having a wide variety of contacts, as well as having accurate descriptions of past events, is helpful in anticipating emergent groups.

Formal and informal structures and interest groups need to be distinguished. The president may formally consult the academic council on budgetary matters, yet informally he or she may actually depend on a few former deans for advice. Identification of formal structures is usually far easier than identification of informal structures. For instance, in universities there is often an implicit prestige system among academic departments in which faculty in "harder," or scientific, fields may take precedence over "softer" fields or vocational or applied fields. Faculty from prestigious fields may dominate committees or administrative assignments. Some departments have traditionally been more involved with campus governance, formally and informally, than others. Observation of leadership patterns and appointments to ad hoc advisory groups often provides clues to these informal structures. The researcher who neglects the informal structures of power and authority may find that in spite of formal approval a proposed change is not implemented or is ineffective.

Special mention needs to be made of the institutional researcher's relationship with the faculty. The presence of a large professional group with an assumed right to share in governance confounds the standard organization analysis of power and authority. Many writers have advocated that the institutional researcher seek faculty status as a way of dealing with this issue. While this may prove useful by acquainting the researcher with students and a large range of faculty, it does not remove the ambiguity of the researcher's position. The institutional researcher is intrinsically part of the administration in spite of courtesy titles or part-time teaching appointments. Without having gone through the tenure review process, the researcher is unlikely to be given equal weight in discussions of academic matters. Generally faculty will enter into many decisions at the institution, and it is not always easy to predict what issues, other than salaries, will attract attention. There is potential for conflict with faculty on a great many issues. Helping to shape faculty opinion by providing data and analysis is far more productive than having to resolve conflict once it has occurred.

Conflict between formal and informal decision making often occurs, and it is fortunate if the institutional researcher can avoid being caught between two competing groups, although this is not always possible. Often information on what significant interest groups on campus are thinking is all that is necessary to modify formal actions, but occasionally appeals to higher authority may be necessary. There are no hard and fast rules about conflict situations, but the institutional researcher's ability to portray all sides of an issue and indicate respective strengths and weaknesses can be useful if the issue has to be referred to a final authority for resolution.

The environmental scan should also identify, as far as possible, the ways in which various interest groups have articulated their points of view in the past and their success in affecting policy. (This review of past behavior may serve as an outline of possible future interest groups and their articulation, but given the fluid nature of academic organizations there can be a wide variation.) Patterns of work for faculty, with leaves, sabbaticals, and changing course assignments, usually result in relatively frequent turnover of faculty participants in both formal and informal interest groups. Predicting future patterns for the articulation and transformation of interest group objectives into policy can be based on these histories, but each new policy issue will change the relevant actors and their influence.

Self-Assessment. Suppose that your institutional research office has conducted an environmental scan and has determined (1) the style of administration, (2) the functions your office routinely fulfills, (3) the relevant formal and informal decision structures at your institution, and (4) the key actors with respect to decisions and issues. The remaining strategic step is to identify the strengths and weaknesses of the institutional research office for your particular institution.

Self-assessment can be done by relying on outside consultants and in-depth questionnaires, but this may be time consuming. It can also be done informally in an afternoon by the director, key staff, and a faculty member or two, for disinterested feedback. Using a panel of observers for evaluation can be very effective in pointing out weaknesses in the operation of the office.

Self-assessment should include analysis of the skills available in the office: modeling, statistical methods, graphic presentation, survey research, and so on. The kinds of data routinely available, the presence of historical series, and the capability for gathering new data all belong in the self-assessment. Parallel with the environmental scan, the self-assessment identifies for the institutional research office itself the style of the office—crisis management and response, or leisurely research.

In addition to a catalogue of skills possessed, the self-assessment needs to evaluate the quality of the performance of the office in each of these areas: What is the record with respect to accuracy, promptness, and completeness of work?

The final step in the process is to match the environmental scan and the self-assessment, and identify places where change is needed. It may be necessary to propose new role functions for your institutional research office if there is a serious difference between what the environmental scan shows and what the office has been doing. The institutional research function may have primarily focused on data gathering, for instance, but the scan may show a need for a more active role in policy analysis.

Developing a Political Strategy: A Few Hints

The self-assessment ought to be directed toward the formulation of a political strategy plan for your institutional research office. This plan should build on strengths identified in the scan and self-assessment.

The major strength of an institutional research office is information and the analysis of information. To the extent that the institutional research office influences the content and flow of information to decision makers, it has influence on the process of arriving at decisions. The weakness inherent in the institutional research function comes from its marginal status: It is in the middle ground, being neither academic nor truly administrative. Since the research office has no operational responsibilities, it must rely on supplying information to others for its influence.

To increase its effectiveness the institutional research office needs to capitalize on this control of information. Centralizing reporting to external agencies allows for consistent data and interpretation. Acting as a clearinghouse for data used in decision making permits analysis on a constant basis and sets data in an overall context. Another specialized function is that of an early warning office. An institutional research office is often uniquely suited to be the early warning office for issues that may become campus crises. Through contracts with peers in other institutions, keeping up with national affairs, and maintaining contacts throughout the campus, the office can often alert relevant campus decision makers to emerging issues. Early warning serves as a useful way to increase the visibility of the institutional research office. Further, because historical information on trends in student interest and other campus activities resides in institutional research offices, "quick and dirty" studies can be done that relate campus history to national trends. Providing the campus statistics to match the *Chronicle of Higher Education*'s Fact File is one example of this function. Trying to anticipate the next decisions or issues that will be considered provides a basis for organizing data collection efforts.

Professional contacts, particularly with institutional researchers in institutions that are used as comparators, are particularly valuable (see Chapter Four). Being able to obtain information quickly on what other institutions are doing enhances the creditability of an institutional research office.

The recent proliferation of state and regional institutional research organizations is a response to some of these needs, and institutional researchers find it increasingly valuable to be well informed about state and regional trends. One potential drawback of the early warning role is that focusing exclusively on extrainstitutional trends without careful consideration of potential internal impacts may result in being perceived as "crying wolf." It is important to assess which issues might actually apply to the institution and to focus only on the most important.

The institutional research office needs also to develop as part of the political strategy plan an approach to unpopular issues, such as the failure rate of certain groups of students, the lack of external funding for faculty in a particular area, or the high unemployment rate for graduates of certain programs. There are some issues that are not popular on campus, but they may still need review and discussion. If the institutional researcher focuses exclusively on such issues, he or she is likely not to be very well received. Getting other groups on campus interested, activating outside constituencies, or building coalitions can be used to begin discussion.

Finally, a complete strategy plan should address the question of providing what is requested versus what is needed. Part of the success of the institutional research office is the ability of the analyst to work with the potential user to define the questions so they can be answered. In this way the institutional research office can make a genuine contribution to solving problems.

It is also useful to know when institutional research does not help, that is, when the question is one of values as opposed to one of data. It may not help to know about the increase in demand of students for entrance into a particular major if in fact there has already been a judgment that the size of this particular major will not be increased. The effective institutional research office points out these problems and issues in such a way that the decision maker is not threatened and separates the issue into questions of fact and statements of preferences.

The strategic plan should also include some thought about the implementation of policy. The institutional researcher is in a unique position to follow up on implementation of policy. Maintaining a network of contacts with administrative officers as well as monitoring institution operations will provide an overview of how implementation is taking place.

Finally, for a quick summary of tactics in the political university, we turn back to Cohen and March for advice: Spend time and energy on issues, persist, exchange status for substance, facilitate opposition participation, overload the system, manage unobtrusively, and finally, volunteer to draft the final report!

References

Balderston, F. E. *Managing Today's University.* San Francisco: Jossey-Bass, 1974.
Baldridge, J. V. *Power and Conflict in the University.* New York: Wiley, 1971.
Baldridge, J. V., Curtis, D. V., Ecker, G. and Riley, G. L. *Policy Making and Effective Leadership.* San Francisco: Jossey-Bass, 1978.
Buhl, L. C., and Lindquist, J. "Academic Improvement Through Action Research." In J. Lindquist (Ed.), *Increasing the Use of Institutional Research.* New Directions for Institutional Research, no. 31. San Francisco: Jossey-Bass, 1981.

Cohen, M. D., and March, J. G. *Leadership and Ambiguity: The American College President.* New York: McGraw-Hill, 1974.

Dressel, P. "Institutional Researchers: Created or Educated?" In R. G. Cope (Ed.), *Professional Development for Institutional Research.* New Directions for Institutional Research, no. 23. San Francisco: Jossey-Bass, 1979.

Haas, R. M. "Winning Acceptance for Institutional Research and Planning." In P. Jedamus, M. W. Peterson, and Associates (Eds.), *Improving Academic Management: A Handbook of Planning and Institutional Research.* San Francisco: Jossey-Bass, 1980.

Hines, E. R., and Hartmark, L. S. *Politics of Higher Education.* AAHE-ERIC Research Report No. 7. Washington, D.C.: American Association for Higher Education, 1980.

Jencks, C., and Riesman, D. *The Academic Revolution.* New York: Doubleday, 1968.

Millett, J. *The Academic Community.* New York: McGraw-Hill, 1962.

Parsons, T., and Platt, G. M. *The American University.* Cambridge, Mass.: Harvard University Press, 1973.

Saupe, J. L., and Montgomery, J. R. *The Nature and Role of Institutional Research... Memo to a College or University.* Tallahassee, Fla.: The Association for Institutional Research, 1970.

Laura E. Saunders is director of planning and capital budget at the University of Washington. She has worked in institutional research since 1968. She is past president of the Pacific Northwest Association for Institutional Research and Planning and is currently a member-at-large of the Association for Institutional Research Executive Committee.

Success in exchanging data with other institutions depends on the purpose of the exchange, the complexity of the data involved, the effort required to participate, and the frequency with which responses are requested.

The Politics of Comparing Data with Other Institutions

Deborah J. Teeter

The idea of exchanges among institutions is not new. Faculty exchanges, student exchanges, cooperative ventures, and research exchanges have all paved the way for data exchanges. Over the past decade, data exchanges have become increasingly popular, undoubtedly due to the information explosion and data-oriented management. Part of the need for comparative data stems from the fact that there are very few well-defined measures of the contributions and outcomes of higher education. Data from other institutions provide management the ability to size up competition, benchmarks for assessing the well-being of their own institutions, the ability to pinpoint areas deserving attention, and guides for policy development. To satisfy increased demands for accountability by local, state, and federal agencies, institutions are using compative data to couch responses in the proper perspective. It is with increasing frequency that comparative data are being used to explain and justify budget requests, salary increases, teaching loads, and tuition increases.

Uses of Comparative Data

More specifically, data from other institutions can be used in making internal budget allocations, examining productivity, or evaluating programs. As financial resources are further constricted by inflation and declining enrollment, faculty productivity data, salary data, and data on support staff can be useful to decision makers when they reallocate financial resources. Because such measures as degree production, research grants, and student–faculty ratios are used frequently as indicators of quality, exchanges of these kinds of data allow some assessment of quality of academic units. Such comparative benchmarks can also serve as a guide or target toward which an institution might strive. Comparative data might also be interesting in the evaluation of the relative funding of an institution. Similar programs might require similar resources, and the perceived quality of a school or program may be directly related to the resources spent on it. Comparative data could be useful not only in internal examinations of an institution but also in external reviews.

University governing bodies, state budget offices, and legislators often use information from other institutions in evaluating budget requests. Comparative data allow them to assess the impact of appropriations relative to the funding of other institutions. For example, salary increases can be evaluated in terms of faculty salaries at peer institutions in order to determine the competitiveness of faculty salaries. The use of comparative data does not imply that a legislature should tie its actions to that of legislatures in other states; rather, comparative data are simply useful tools to the legislator in evaluating budget requests.

Another related use of exchanged data is to address accountability and credibility problems. For example, a newly proposed program might be more credible and readily acceptable if it can be demonstrated that other institutions have established similar programs. Moreover, with the increased emphasis on accountability, particularly by the federal government, it is important that like institutions respond to accountability requirements in a similar manner. This similarity in responding enhances the responses of all the institutions and allows a more reasonable and consistent evaluation of the required data.

Reasons for Cooperation

In spite of the merits and uses of comparative data, motivating institutions to participate in an information exchange can be very demanding. A number of factors should be taken into account by the institution trying to decide whether to participate in a data exchange: (1) the institution requesting assistance might be able to return the favor in the future, (2) it might be desirable to be compared with the school requesting data, (3) the results of the data may be desirable, (4) it is a professional courtesy to assist a sister institution, and (5) it may be politically expedient to cooperate.

For example, a request for data from a prestigious institution to one of lesser stature would probably be honored simply for the benefits of being associated with that institution in its study. Furthermore, comparisons that point out deficiencies in an institution compared with institutions perceived as of higher quality or better funded might be desirable. Some institutions may want to demonstrate superior faculty salaries and choose comparisons accordingly. On the other hand, those same comparisons might be very valuable to a competitively disadvantaged institution to demonstrate to its funders the need for more resources to compete with similar institutions.

Providing data for reasons of political expediency may be a concession to the fact that at times it is easier to give someone what they want rather than suffer the consequences. State and federal agencies often wield a large stick that encourages cooperation in data collection even when it may not be relevant. For example, an intrastate comparison of cost-per-credit-hour data of all institutions within a system in which many are significantly different from one another in size, mission, and funding may have little meaning.

The Nature of Information Exchanged

Most frequently exchanged among institutions are data—facts and figures—about a particular topic. Enrollment, appropriations and financial data, faculty salaries, tenure policies, and general policies and procedures are frequently of interest to other schools. Comparisons of these kinds allow for answers to questions such as "How well are we doing as compared to institution X?" For example, enrollment trends in a particular discipline might be of great interest to an institution that is experiencing declines it believes to be counter to national or regional trends. This kind of information helps determine if a problem is local or of a more general nature. As more and more states encounter financial difficulties, information about how institutions in those states are coping with financial problems could be very helpful to those who have yet to experience the same kinds of financial crises.

The kinds of data frequently exchanged about faculty includes not only salary information but also tenure percentages and sabbatical leave policies. Student-faculty ratios and faculty activity analyses are examples where comparative data substitute for well-defined measures of faculty workload and productivity. While ratios and rates can be calculated, it is often difficult to interpret these statistics meaningfully. However, information from similar institutions can indicate whether these ratios and rates approach the norm and, if they do not, whether additional investigation is warranted.

Since institutions are frequently subject to the same governmental regulations, it might be useful to exchange approaches to meeting these requirements. An example of such an exchange was the need to develop procedures to meet the requirements of the Office of Management and Budget Circular A-21 regarding indirect cost recovery on federal grants. Informal polls of how other institutions were responding to the A-21 requirements were common and those institutions who had decided how to meet the A-21 requirements were often willing to share with others details of their proposed procedures.

Research findings and analysis on a particular topic might also be exchanged. Since the enrollment picture is unclear, institutions are increasingly seeking means of retaining current students as well as attracting new students. Similar institutions are often able to borrow research findings from one another and to apply or implement recommendations without redundantly conducting the same research. Furthermore, special research projects can be both time consuming and costly, and often a school may need to respond quickly and may not have time or resources to do its own research. While borrowing other institutions' data may be somewhat risky, careful examination and application of research findings at other institutions could save time and money.

Exchange Mechanism

In contemplating an exchange of information, a number of factors should be considered to assure the likelihood of a successful exchange and to enhance the usefulness of the data.

One-Way Data Exchange. One type of data exchange might be characterized as a one-way exchange. In this kind of exchange, all the benefits accrue to the institution requesting the data. In this case, the requesting party desires information from another institution, but the institution providing the data has no interest in similar information from the requesting institution. One might even consider the effort a data collection rather than an exchange. Most institutions encounter these kinds of data requests and undoubtedly respond to them for reasons discussed earlier.

Ad hoc data exchanges allow a particular problem or issue to be explored in a timely manner. Thus institutions initiating ad hoc data exchanges should take care not to wear out their welcome with institutions from whom they are requesting data. To minimize the impact of ad hoc data exchanges, the requesting institution should consider utilizing established reports or be willing to manipulate raw data into the desired format. Any effort to reduce the burden of the data exchange upon an institution promotes cooperation and increases the likelihood of a successful data exchange.

An example of a one-way exchange might include an institution requesting information about a particular topic such as the operation of financial aid offices. These kinds of requests usually have a specific focus and the data requested are geared to a particular need. Often the information that is gathered is not of interest to anyone other than the requesting institution. The information does, however, meet a particular need and can only be acquired through the cooperation of other institutions.

Two-Way Data Exchange. The second type of exchange encountered is a two-way exchange in which both parties benefit from the data exchanged. Mutual data exchanges often involve the joint development of data formats, data definitions, and procedures that enhance the comparability of the data exchanged. Furthermore, in two-way exchanges, more complicated data are likely to be exchanged than in one-way exchanges, because both parties have an interest in the information.

Data Exchange Networks. Data exchange networks help avoid the duplication of effort generated by redundant requests for data. This is particularly useful among a group of institutions who are interested in the same data. Rather than face multiple requests for similar data, an institution can provide common data to a number of schools in a consistent and timely manner. Additionally, routine exchanges of mutually agreed-upon data allow for the preparation of the data in an orderly manner. After paying the start-up costs of organizing the data according to mutually agreed-upon formats, the annual maintenance cost should be minimal. Routine data exchanges also provide a baseline of data which will allow trend analysis. Lastly, data exchange networks often have explicit guidelines about the use of exchanged information and, in particular, about sharing semipublic data with third parties. Such guidelines also further the cause of interinstitutional cooperation, since institutions have some assurance as to how their data will be handled.

Scope of Data Exchanges. The scope of data exchanges covers a continuum from "quick and dirty" data preparation through regularly prepared data to exchanges of raw data gathered into previously agreed-upon formats by either the requester or the requestee. "Quick and dirty" exchanges usually consist of simple facts and figures, such as enrollment counts, number of faculty, tuition charges, and total budget. In some cases, a requester is able to gather the desired data from readily available sources provided by the requestee, such as Higher Education General Information Survey (HEGIS) reports and internal salary studies. Such exchanges limit the workload placed upon the cooperating institution. More complex data exchanges may require that the responding institution go to considerable effort to provide the desired data. Most frustrating to responding institutions are data requests that ask for data in aggregations totally unlike those used by the responding school. These requests take considerable time to gather and prepare.

Gathering the Data. Once the inquiring institution has identified data to be gathered, there are a number of ways in which to acquire the information. Telephone surveys are used frequently in collecting "quick and dirty" data. This approach appears to work particularly well when requestors call institutions with whom a data exchange network has already been established, because it is presumed that the reliability of the data gathered over the telephone is good when one is speaking with a person who is known. Another technique for gathering data is the use of printed questionnaires and/or surveys. Such surveys often require more time and effort both for the preparer and respondent than a telephone survey. Salary surveys are often conducted by questionnaires. The use of questionnaires allows a variety of topics to be explored. such as athletic programs, space use, federal research funding, and auxiliary enterprises.

Another means for gathering data is at meetings of mutual interest. Professional meetings in particular provide an excellent opportunity to discuss and exchange data about common concerns. For this to be an effective means of data exchange, there must be an agreed-upon format, a mechanism for analyzing data and returning the results to participating institutions, and a perceived mutual benefit on the part of the participating schools. Another technique for gathering information is visits to the institutions from which data are desired. This is a costly and involved process that may be necessary when the data requirements are extensive or when it is assumed that it is unreasonable to place such heavy data collection requirements on the institution from whom the information is sought. Of course, such visits require the cooperation of the institution providing data, but have the advantage that the requesting institution assumes the burden of gathering the required material.

Choosing Institutions for Data Exchanges. Selecting institutions with which to exchange data should be guided by the purpose for which the data will be used. Furthermore, the source of the data has to be credible to those who will ultimately use the data.

One method for choosing institutions with which to compare data is the use of informed judgments; the collective wisdom of those who will be utilizing the data guides the selection of peers. This is particularly appropriate when the data will be used internally, and the selection of peers does not require extensive justification. A more rigorous and objective process might be necessary if the exchanged data will be used to support external budget requests. Several objective processes have been developed (for instance, Terenzini and others, 1980; Elsass and Lingenfelter, 1980; McCoy, 1980; Smart, Martin, Elton, 1980; Rawson, Hoyt, and Teeter, forthcoming). These processes use available data, such as enrollment statistics, degree production data, and budget and expenditure data, to cluster institutions sharing similar characteristics. Some procedures are more elaborate than others, but the bottom line in all of them is to assess similarity of institutions using some objective criteria.

Another process for selecting peers is the use of established groups such as the members of the Association of American Universities (AAU), the National Association for State Universities and Land Grant Colleges (NASULGC), and the Council for the Advancement of Small Colleges (CASC). Members of such groups, by definition, should have common characteristics and might be very appropriate peer groups, once again depending upon the purpose of the data exchange.

Using Peer Groups

The University of Kansas (KU) has defined several peer groups for different purposes. Several that will be discussed briefly are (1) formula funding, (2) the NCHEMS major research universities (MRU) Task Force, (3) the Association of American Universities Data Exchange (AAUDE), and (4) Big Eight institutions.

The formula funding peer group consists of five institutions besides KU. It was established to develop a benchmark to analyze state funding requests by mapping the peer data into the KU operating framework and then comparing KU expenditures with the average of the peers. Due to the budgetary impact of this analysis, the peers were carefully selected, using both subjective and objective criteria. Accordingly, this group shares more similarities than any other group with which KU compares itself—they are true peers. Since the financial data required to support the funding formulas are very extensive and detailed, it was decided to collect data on site to minimize the burden on the participating institutions. This is an example of one-way data exchange, though effort has been made to make the data useful to the peer institutions.

The politics of this gathering effort have varied by school as might be expected. Two institutions had as much to gain from the data analysis as KU, one institution was relatively indifferent, and two had no interest whatsoever in the analysis. In this case, those institutions that were relatively better funded than the average of the group had little interest in the data. Furthermore, one institution did not even want the comparative analysis shared with them. On the other hand, those peers at the other end of the spectrum wanted to use the results for the same reason KU was collecting the data — to support budget requests.

After establishing a working relationship, rapport was cultivated by routinely reviewing the data analysis with each institution to ensure appropriate treatment of each instituion's data. Wherever possible, KU transformed each peer school's raw idea into the KU expenditure structure rather than requesting that the institution perform the task. In one case, an institution had not assigned course levels (lower division undergraduate, upper division undergraduate, graduate I, graduate II) to each course; such assignments were crucial to the analysis. KU used course data that specified levels of students enrolled to assign a level to each course.

The NCHEMS Task Force was another data exchange group of which the University of Kansas was a member. This group was formed to explore the appropriateness and application of NCHEMS information exchange procedures (IEP) to major research universities. Each participating university had been mandated to implement IEP. Since institutions actively sought involvement in this project, cooperation was not an issue.

It became apparent very quickly, however, that there were some very real differences in the institutions, even though they all were major research universities. Several institutions were very large, and one was not only the major public institution in the state but also the land grant institution. Furthermore, the task of this group was to map each institution's data into a common format, unlike any one institution's in particular. While this approach did not completely stymie the process, it made it more difficult and time consuming. It was possible during the course of this effort for one institution to learn as much about another as it knew about itself. Under different circumstances, that could have been a very threatening situation. These kinds of projects require considerable time, effort, and expenditures, and might cause one to think twice before becoming involved in a similar effort.

Since each institution had strong reasons for participating, cooperation was never an issue, nor was there a lack of candor in the deliberations. This contrasts with the formula funding project, in which cooperation must be continually and diplomatically solicited, since the participating schools are cooperating only at KU's request.

The oldest data exchange group in which the University of Kansas participates is the AAUDE. This is an example of using members of an established group—the Association of American Universities—to form a data exchange network. Institutions participate by choice, and the scope of activities is extensive. Institutions routinely exchange data on salaries, student credit hours, graduate student stipends, fringe benefits, and other things. The responsibilities for using the data are well defined, including the sharing of data with third parties. Most of the data exchange has become routine and accordingly requires minimal effort in the annual reporting to the other institutions.

This group is a collection of true, and desirable, peers for KU. In this case, *desirable* translates to those institutions to which KU aspires to achieve comparable academic quality and levels of funding. Depending on the need for comparable data, KU on occasion uses a subset of the institutions participating in the exchange, rather than the data from all institutions. In justifying salary increases, KU usually looks at the salaries of the schools located in the Midwest, since that is more politically salient.

The politics of this group is not dissimilar to the NCHEMS-MRU peer group. Self-selection is the key to cooperation, but once an institution agrees to participate, it assumes certain obligations and responsibilities. Politeness generally prevails, but when appropriate, good-natured chastisement is ordered for those failing to adhere to agreed-upon time schedules, formats, and definitions.

The newest data exchange group in which KU participates is the Big Eight. The Big Eight is an athletic conference rather than a collection of schools identified for academic reasons, such as the AAUDE. Historically, KU has been reluctant to be involved in routine data exchanges with this group for several reasons: (1) In the past, these exchanges have been ad hoc, with no formal mechanism to facilitate the exchange of information; (2) five of the eight are land-grant institutions with different missions from that of KU; and (3) previous exchanges of information with these schools have not been advantageous to KU. However, the regional proximity of the Big Eight schools and KU's funding sources' familiarity with them has increased the demand for the collection of comparative data. Therefore, KU is now promoting exchange activities where in the recent past it was discouraging them.

In summary, success in exchanging data with other institutions depends on the purpose of the exchange, the complexity of the data involved, the effort required to participate, and the frequency with which responses are requested. In addition, the sensitivity of the requesting institution as to the impact that the request will have on the responding school is critical. In the final analysis, common sense, diplomacy, and selling the responding institution on the benefits of participating in an exchange with one's institution are the factors that will assure a successful exchange.

References

Bloom, A. M., and Montgomery, J. R. "Conducting Data Exchange Programs." *The AIR Professional File,* no. 5. Tallahassee, Fla.: The Association for Institutional Research, 1980.

Elsass, J. E., and Lingenfelter, P. E. "An Identification of College and University Peer Groups." In D. J. Collier (Ed.), *Innovations in Higher Education Management: Coping with the 1980s.* Boulder, Colo.: National Center for Higher Education Management Systems, 1980.

Kansas Board of Regents. *Formula Funding at the Kansas Board of Regents Institutions.* (Pamphlet). 1979.

McCoy, M. "Selection of Similar or Peer Institutions Among the Major Doctoral Institutions in the U.S., Preliminary Results." Boulder, Colo.: National Center for Higher Education Management Systems, 1980.

Rawson, T. M., Hoyt, D. P., and Teeter, D. J. "Identifying 'Comparable' Institutions." *Research in Higher Education,* forthcoming.

Smart, J. C., Martin, R. O., and Elton, C. F. "Qualitative and Conventional Indices of Benchmark Institutions." *Proceedings.* Atlanta, Ga.: Association for Institutional Research, 1980.

Terenzini, P. T., Hartmark, L., Lorang, W. G., Jr., and Shirley, R. C. "A Conceptual and Methodological Approach to the Identification of Peer Institutes." *Research in Higher Education,* 1980, *12,* 347–364.

Deborah J. Teeter is director of the Office of Institutional Research and Planning at the University of Kansas. She has served in institutional research positions for the past ten years.

How can institutional administrators more favorably influence the policy actions of state agencies?

The Politics of Dealing with State Agencies— An Institutional View

E. Grady Bogue

Politics is "the art or science concerned with guiding or influencing governmental policy." The conciseness of Webster's may not do justice to libraries of political science. It does, however, furnish a direct entree to the theme of this chapter. Our questions are simple. How can institutional administrators more favorably influence the policy actions of state agencies, such as coordinating councils, commissions, and boards? What values and what actions offer promise of more constructive relationships with these agencies?

Given the variety of institutional and state agency relationships— for instance, authority patterns, performance history, state fiscal conditions, staffing patterns and abilities—one can expect the art of influence to be a complex one. However, an analysis of institutional and state agency roles and the experience of seasoned administrators reveal a set of ideals helpful to others.

Artistic practice begins with knowledge. Our purpose in this chapter is to present ideas and experiences that will improve the art of influence with state agencies. The chapter will close with an examination of future issues that may affect campus and state agency relationships.

Needs and Resources in Tension

In preparing this chapter, several college presidents and institutional research officers in different states were interviewed. A common point of counsel was for campus administrators to more fully appreciate the complex role of state agencies. A good argument can be made for reciprocity on this point. For the moment, however, let's examine the role of state agencies.

The Boundary Role. In an earlier volume of the *New Directions for Institutional Research* series, the role of state agencies was described as follows:

> The theory of state planning and coordinating agencies involves several assumptions. First, more effective and objective planning is expected from staffs having sensitivity to the special character of higher education, but having no operating responsibility for particular institutions. Second, these agencies are expected to take a long-range view of policy decisions, to make decisions, and to render counsel without undue influence of political expediency. Third, the legal authority of the agency is usually vested in a lay commission or council to provide a balance of professional insight and lay oversight. Finally, the decisions and recommendations of these state agencies are subject to review, revision, and rejection by legislatures, providing a check on their purposes and performance.
>
> State planning and coordinating agencies were born in compromise and live in dissent. It is difficult business working the boundary between institutional-board expectations for advocacy and executive-legislative expectations for accountability (Bogue, 1980, pp. 69-70).

The extent to which state agencies live in dissent is evidenced by continued critique (Elliot, 1982; Enarson, 1980) and the frequency with which bills are submitted in state legislatures to increase, to delimit, and to delete their roles.

The concept of a boundary agency is important for any campus administrator to appreciate. State agencies are caught in the cross fire of institutional officers, who project legitimate needs, and executive or

legislative officers, who have limited resources to allocate. Needs and resources are in constant tension. Sitting on this academic picket fence is not made any easier by these factors:
- Declining fiscal resources at both state and federal levels
- The prospect of declining enrollments on some campuses
- The growing proclivity of state legislatures to tag appropriations bills with other requirements that are controlling in nature (American Association of State Colleges and Universities, 1982)
- The growing involvement of state fiscal officers in questions of institutional management
- The tension in many states over the allocation of state dollars to private institutions
- The potential for increased competitiveness among institutions if enrollments decrease
- A continuing federal interest in desegregation and employment issues.

One of the state agency critiques earlier cited (Elliot, 1982) opens with the headlines "Are Coordinating Boards Needed Anymore?" Among several interesting but not very helpful analogies presented in the critique is the following: "The working mechanisms of large universities are fine, handcrafted clocks. Like such clocks, when left to good clockmakers, they tend to do what they are supposed to do and to last almost forever" (p. 64).

Fine clockmakers and the clocks they make do not usually engage in questionable ethical practices. A few college administrators and their faculty do. They are invited to appear before legislative committees because of extensive audit exceptions. They are cited for neglect of building maintenance and abuse of travel funds. They are placed on probation for improper administration of federal aid funds. They are taken to court for inaction or wrongheaded action on affirmative employment practices. They are sanctioned for shady activity in intercollegiate athletics.

More critical and damaging to higher education—and also atypical of fine clockmakers—are more fundamental ethical difficulties related to the heart of our college and university communities. These have also been discussed in an earlier volume of the *New Directions for Institutional Research* series:

> (1) A university adopts an "experimental" admissions policy the first year after it suffers its first enrollment decline in twenty

years. (2) A community college gives academic credit for national guard drill without prior knowledge of the participants. (3) A graduate department in a major university lowers admission requirements for doctoral work the first year after it lost two faculty positions because of declining enrollments. (4) A college fails to execute its academic retention policy and state auditors find over 100 students enrolled who are academically ineligible.

While federal and state agencies have intruded into financial and personnel practices, they have not, on a broad basis, disturbed fundamental academic policy questions of who gets in (admissions), who stays in (retention), who gets out (graduation). Whether these decisions will remain the primary domain of institutions and their faculties is a critical question. (Bogue, 1980, p. 72).

In the face of these past abuses and current issues, there does not appear to be a trend on the part of legislatures to dismantle state agencies. Recent trends in the authority accorded to state agencies would certainly not suggest any lessening of their role.

More important, legislatures and governors established state agencies and still need them for reasoned and objective counsel of the complex issues of mission, finance, and performance in higher education. If not provided by state agencies, such counsel will be provided by growing legislative staff, who may not have as much experience or sensitivity as state agency personnel.

Does this mean that state agencies warrant our uncritical allegience? It does not. There are too many depressing cases of insensitive leadership there as well:
- Imbalanced concerns about legislative interests to the neglect of campus
- Preparation of reports for legislative consumption that lack proper critique by campus officers, producing legislative decisions based on inadequate data
- Release of reports to public press and legislative officers before they are seen by campus officials
- Unwillingness to show as much policy courage before legislative councils and committees as before campus officers
- Quantitative analyses that unfairly mask important differences in history and environments among campuses

- Data and reporting demands on campuses that allow inadequate time for preparation and that lack clarity of decision application
- Expression of vested interest among lay officials who are expected to act in the best interest of all institutions
- Professional staff who have technical competence but who lack the appreciation that comes from having served on a campus.

Campus and state agency officers should not be throwing rocks at one another. Constructive relationships come with mutual respect and sensitivity and the willingness to both teach and learn.

Attitudes and Realities in State Agency Relationships

Believing is seeing. No principle of human relations is better supported in social behavioral research than this. The quality of our expectations is a prime determinant in the quality of behavior elicited from others (Livingston, 1969; Rosenthal, 1973). Our expectations may not endow colleagues with abilities they do not have to take wrongdoing from them. Our expectations may, however, lift the vision and initiative of colleagues.

The lesson is clear. If campus administrators believe that state agencies were created to thwart the legitimate aspirations of campuses, their behavior will have a different flavor than it would if they saw a legitimate and complementary role for state agencies. If campus executives and their staff see the state agency staff as having less intellectual credentials than they have, this condescending attitude is likely to generate behavior less contributing to good relationships that their looking for the best in state agency colleagues.

This theme was nicely stated by a college president who had also served as a state agency executive: "There is always a temptation to build up a we and them syndrome that, whether intended or not, leads to pitting the internal faculty and staff of an institution against the people connected with a state agency. Blame is sometimes shifted to the external people and this tactic leads to division and very often decisions by the state which are not helpful for the institution" (Albright, 1981).

Another president commenting on attitudes indicated that "I prefer long-term values which are accomplished by the simple process of gaining respect and trust. If officers in those situations believe me and trust me, I don't have to protest so loudly and so frequently" (Vail, 1981).

An institutional research officer with significant national and institutional experience suggested, "my one point of counsel is to be responsive, honest, and candid.... To put the counsel in other terms, it is to display with the coordinating board folk the same high degree of integrity we expect of colleges and universities in all their endeavors" (Saupe, 1981).

Why is there this need to emphasize the golden rule of human relationships? Perhaps these experienced campus administrators have seen these values too often violated.

What are some of the attitudes and values needing our attention? Here are some of those that might enhance the art of influence with state agencies.

Candor. How many new academic program proposals have been submitted to state agencies indicating that the costs necessary to implement the program were minimal or zero? In how many cases did the rhetoric of the proposal correspond to reality? And what do such proposals say for institutional candor? State agency personnel are sensitive, and properly so, to the integrity of institutional promises. Did the institution seek the approval of a new option, track, or concentration that looked more like a full major when it appeared in its catalogue? What does this say for candor with state agency personnel and with students?

The ability to influence state agency personnel is not enhanced by dishonesty in relationships. An academic officer of a state coordinating agency reports having reviewed and evaluated two campus proposals for master's degrees. Both promised the immediate employment of Ph.D. level faculty to augment existing staff once the program was approved. An external consultant team agreed on by both campuses and the state agency endorsed the need for these faculty. The programs were approved and implemented. Only one campus followed through in the manner promised, however. That campus found its later proposals moving along with a little more certainty and swiftness than the other.

In another example, the relatively weak correspondence between institutional catalogue statements of major programs in an institution and the official program inventory maintained by one state higher education agency led the agency staff to work with governing board and campus staff in bringing additional clarity to catalogue statements. The inaccuracies and ambiguities in the catalogue were recognized and admitted. Consequently, the agency inquiry encouraged long overdue improvement in the institution's statement of authorized degrees, majors, and submajors.

The negotiated outcome was the publication in each institutional catalogue of an outline showing approved degrees, majors, and submajors (options, concentrations, tracks, and so on). This particular exchange between campus and state agency suggests another value, the one of creative tension.

Creative Tension. It has been suggested that campus administrators should understand the constructive role of creative tension. Under proper tension muscles become stronger. Without any tension, they become flabby and weak. Under too much tension, their functional use can be destroyed. A careful translation of this concept to human relationships is instructive. We should expect some tension between campus and state agency.

Properly balanced, this tension can have useful outcomes. The compromise on catalogue program statements previously cited is a good illustration. Though the state agency probe into the accuracy of catalogue statements provided some irritation to institutional governing boards and to campus staffs, it led to a beneficial outcome. The benefit, however, was realized more clearly after some time had elapsed.

Compromise. Campus executives should remember that they have to live with themselves and state agencies tomorrow as well as today. Letting all ride on a single decision suggests that we have only one half of wisdom. The willingness to seek compromise and to suggest and explore alternative solutions is often important.

Following is an illustration of compromise offered by a college president. His campus sought the approval of two new degrees at the professional level in the arts—a Master of Fine Arts and a Master of Music degree. The campus already offered Master of Arts degrees in both these fields, as well as a Master of Science in teaching, a matter of some concern to the state agency staff and director. To acquire the new degrees, which were deemed more important to the future of the campus and its mission, the institution agreed to relinquish the old degree majors—a decision not totally satisfying to either the campus or the state agency but one acceptable to both and one that provided room for educational progress as viewed by both the campus and the state agency.

Respect. This is a word used frequently by campus administrators. Let us return to the "great expectations" theme that opened this discussion on attitudes. One campus executive offered this conviction:

"There is a strong temptation to regard bureaucrats with some scorn as professional and intellectual inferiors.... It behooves us to work with the people who work there rather than someone we might wish were there. Working with them involves treating them with respect commensurate with the office and responsibility they hold" (Vail, 1981).

It is generally felt that staff working in state agencies should have been in the academic trenches, that is, that they should have experience at the campus level before taking state policy responsibility. There is, however, a bit of arrogance in this view, because it suggests that the only way to gain educational and campus sensitivity is by working there. This is not so. Just one state agency autocrat who has served at the campus level or just one capable executive at the state level who has not should keep us open on this point.

For campus administrators, it may be well to remember that there is intelligence of mind, heart, and hand. Laplace was a great French mathematician. But the French government almost went broke when he took over the financial reins of government. The intelligence required for magnificent analytical and artistic advances at the campus level may not be the same kind of intelligence required for the complex and controversial working of government. There is no room for mediocrity at either place.

Influencing Actions

Attitudes are heralds of action. Thus, some actions that might influence state agency decisions more favorably are implicit in the previous discussion. The politics of other actions is not very mysterious.

Proposal Timing and Completeness. Colleges and universities develop reputations with their students and their communities. In banks and barber shops, in concerts and churches, and in supermarkets and motels, the standards and expectations of our campuses are known, discussed, and communicated among those we serve. We also forge reputations in the eyes of state agency staff. One of the more important ways is in the quality of staff work and proposals submitted to these agencies:

- Are proposals and other reports submitted on time?
- Are they complete and accurate?
- Are they written clearly and concisely?

State agency staff know which institutions are more likely to submit thoroughly prepared academic program proposals—with concise and fully prepared statements of need with evidence to back them up, complete faculty information, carefully considered curriculum outlines, honest statements of anticipated costs. State agency staff know which institutions can be expected to submit good fiscal proposals—with accurate statements of anticipated income and expenditure patterns that are likely to match requests. If we want state agency staff to be our advocates more than our adversaries, we must equip them to be our advocate with carefully and thoroughly prepared proposals and reports.

Proposals and Personalities. Fact and feeling are components of most decisions at the state and at the campus. State agency staff are no different from other decision makers. They find it easier to have confidence in those they know and easier to be suspicious of those they do not. They will make sterile decisions when they have no knowledge beyond data on a piece of paper and when they are not familiar with the people and the institution. They do not like surprises, and they appreciate being involved early in major and critical decisions.

A small but highly effective gesture of goodwill, therefore, is to have state agency staff on your campus. This provides a pleasant opportunity for them to know your people, your campus and its mission, and your community. The active cultivation of state agency staff by counterpart institutional officers—academic, fiscal, and so on—is a common sense step. Invite the entire agency—its lay members and staff—to hold meetings on your campus. Campus administrators should encourage state agencies to get out of the capital city and be on the campuses for which they are responsible.

Conversely, there is no reason why campus executives and administrators should not meet state agency staff and lay members on their own turf. Informal visits with staff or board members can frequently transform adversaries to advocates. Misunderstandings concerning particular issues can be laid aside. Occasionally a touch of courage and courtesy can gain new ground.

Management Competence and Integrity. Given the content of previous discussion, this point of counsel may appear redundant. There are few actions more helpful in state agency relationships than simply doing our jobs well. A reputation for high-quality educational programs, for truth on both promise and delivery to our students and communities, and for competence and integrity in management is built a step at a time. It can be seriously undermined with a single careless or unethical act.

Submitting good proposals, having state agency staff on campus, and taking community leaders to hearings will not be of much help if your institution has just been cited for audit exceptions, if one of your major programs has just had its accreditation withdrawn, if you failed to hire faculty or furnish other resources pledged, or if the federal government has taken you to court for abuse of aid programs.

Orchestration of Community Support. "Among the things that make it easier for agencies to act favorably on requests is the development of strong public support for institutional goals—support that is not directly connected with specific issues, but that strongly endorses the general direction of the institution" (Thornton, 1981). This is a theme needing sensitive attention.

An institution that has cultivated the long-term goodwill of its community through high-quality educational and service programs can and should call upon that community goodwill in relationships with state agencies. If it is carefully orchestrated, there is no reason why community support should not also be focused on specific decisions.

Community support must be used with sensitivity, however. Carefully chosen letters of support for academic, fiscal, and capital proposals can be a wise tactic, for example. Too many letters can generate an overkill response among state agency staff and lay members. The orchestration of public statements from community leaders is also appropriate. One or two well-worded statements from the right persons can sometimes be as effective as a room full of community advocates. Private and informal meetings with staff can often be more effective than pressure brought in public. Community leaders who carry a chip on their shoulder for state agencies and who approach hearings in an adversary frame of mind may do more harm than good.

It is incumbent upon the institution to know the complexity of the decision being engaged and its impact beyond the institution. This knowledge and sensitive display of community support will distinguish the artist from the mechanic in the politics of state agency relationships.

Under what circumstances, for example, does a campus or its governing board take an issue beyond the state agency—to the courts or to the legislature? No act is more filled with risk than this. State agencies appreciate no more than campus executives those who take issues around them. While referral of a decision that has already been treated by the state agency may be more defensible, it pays to test the risks and benefits there as well.

This is not a counsel of timidity. There are times when it is essential to test the authority of the state agency vis-à-vis the campus or its governing board, and all should realize that a test is needed. There are also times when the legislature might well become the forum for issue resolution. When one issue is taken to the legislature, however, it may be more difficult to keep others at home.

An example of principles in tension recently emerged in Louisiana. Following earlier statewide studies of undergraduate teacher preparation programs, the Louisiana Board of Regents, the state coordinating and planning agency, adopted in June 1981 a policy requiring students seeking entrance to teacher education to have a grade point average of 2.2 and a score of 16 on the ACT. The state legislature had previously passed an act requiring a minimum grade point average of 2.2.

As a constitutional agency, the board of regents has the authority to revise, terminate, and approve academic programs. The key word is to "revise." As reported in an earlier issue of the *New Directions for Institutional Research* series (Bogue, 1980), the Board of Regents has terminated a number of programs. They had not, however, engaged the state's three governing boards and their respective campuses on an issue of admissions standards—at least in a legal test of authority.

The Southern University Board of Supervisors, which operates three historically black campuses, took the position that this act by the board of regents was discriminatory and an infringement on the proper powers of the governing board. In early 1982, the board of regents entered a lawsuit to test this authority issue. The lawsuit was placed against the Southern University Board of Supervisors. At the time of this writing, the Louisiana State University Board of Supervisors has empowered its president to intervene on the side of Southern University, though no legal action has been filed at this moment.

This is a good example of a prickly issue. Though the regents' policy has the potential for limiting the number of black entrants to teacher education, many argue that the policy intent of the board of regents is needed to improve teacher education programs. Others indicate that there is already an output quality control for teacher education in the form of a qualifying score on the National Teacher Examination required for state certification.

The setting of admission standards is, however, an educational authority historically assumed by governing boards and generally delegated to campus faculties. Its good intent notwithstanding, if a state agency—which is not a governing board—has the authority to set admissions standards and otherwise revise academic programs, then the authority of the governing board and its respective campus faculties in matters of educational practice and standards is certainly in serious question. The governing board becomes little more than a procedural passageway between its campuses and the state agency.

Perhaps a good way to close this discussion would be to ask if there are some actions campus administrators should avoid. Some of these are implicit in the previous discussion. They are made more explicit in this counsel from a college president:

> There are some tactics I do counsel against. The first is deception. Never ask for a new program on the grounds that it will cost nothing. Never ask for something you cannot use. Never promise something you do not intend to deliver.
>
> The second is intimidation. A regrettable fact is that officials of state government often are expected to have knowledge, talents, and memories far beyond anything we have a right to expect. Thus, an understanding approach has a chance of working, while a threatening approach can intimidate.
>
> The third refers to buck passing. A constant charging of all evils to state officials is ultimately demeaning to all. The executive who cannot be a part of the state's team but who must blame everything on state officials creates a problem for those officials. Equally important, however, is the impression fixed locally that the executive has no authority and no clout. He undermines himself [Vail, 1981].

Another president offers this piece of cautious counsel: "It does not seem to me to be good practice for a chief executive to hound agency members or staff incessantly with a lot of detail and repeated bombardment of what can come to be considered childish insistence upon a piece of candy" (Albright, 1981).

Deception, intimidation, buck passing, childish insistence—this is behavior not likely to promote the art of influence with state agencies. Do the good guys—the ones who avoid deception and intimidation, and so on—always win? Perhaps not in the short run. We are not working for the short run, however. Presidents, institutional researchers, and other administrators are important, but temporary, in the life of a magnificent and precious instrument in our society. Colleges and universities are trustees of humanity's more noble values. How sad it would be to defame the values we hold in trust.

Higher Education on the Offensive

What lies ahead for campus and state agency relationships? The promise of additional tension is high, and the need for statesmen is great. Earlier possible stresses that are obvious to any campus or state agency executives were mentioned: uneasy fiscal climates from state and federal levels, enrollment uncertainties and possible increased competition among campuses for students, the temptation to lower educational standards, the intrusion of legislative and executive officers into governing board and campus authority, and the possible conflict of authority among campuses, state agencies, and legislative-executive officers.

Here are some of the issues and questions that promise a lively climate for campuses, state agencies, and legislative-executive officers in the next few years:

1. Will legislators and governors look to state agencies for more help on capital outlay requests? In those states having coordinating and planning agencies, academic and fiscal allocation decisions have been largely delegated to state agencies. Capital outlay decisons tend to remain highly politicized. Will state treasury conditions encourage legislators and governors to endow state agencies with more responsibility on capital outlay in the future?

2. Will there be additional conflicts between legislative-executive officers and governing boards over the management authority of boards? Can a governor or finance/administration commissioner fix the salary of a campus executive, or is that solely a governing board prerogative?

3. Will legislative-executive offices continue to develop staffs for conducting program as well as fiscal audits of campuses?

4. Will formula funding based on enrollments prove as useful in a time of enrollment decrease as increase?

5. Will legislators and governors begin to impose upon higher education acts designed to control quality, as they have done for public elementary and secondary education? *The question is not academic* and not trivial!

6. Will voluntary accreditation retain its quality assurance role or will states take on more of this role?

Constructive resolution of these and other future issues requires that campus administrators and faculty be on the offensive—before they get put on the defensive. That offensive should include elements of attitude and action outlined in this chapter. Educational quality and management integrity are foundation elements. These acts and attitudes will enhance not only our relationships with state agencies but strengthen our ability to retain the independence and diversity essential to the future strength of our campuses. The ultimate and most important beneficiaries are our students.

References

Albright, A. D. Letter from the president of Northern Kentucky University to author, November 10, 1981.
American Association of State Colleges and Universities. Memo to the president, December 29, 1981, p. 7.
Bogue, E. G. "State Agency Approaches to Academic Program Evaluation." In E. Craven (Ed.), *Academic Program Evaluation.* New Directions for Institutional Research, no. 27. San Francisco: Jossey-Bass, 1980.
Elliott, P. G. "Are Coordinating Boards Needed Anymore?" *The Chronicle of Higher Education,* January 13, 1982, p. 64.
Enarson, H. "Quality and Accountability: Are We Destroying What We Want to Preserve?" *Change Magazine,* October 1980, pp. 7-10.
Livingston, J. S. "Pygmalion in Management." *Harvard Business Review,* July-August 1969, pp. 81-89.
Rosenthal, R. "The Pygmalion Effect Lives." *Psychology Today,* September 1973, p. 58.
Saupe, J. L. Letter from the director of institutional research, University of Missouri, to author, December 21, 1981.
Thornton, R. Letter from the president of Arkansas State University to author. November 19, 1981.
Vail, C. B. Letter from the president of Winthrop College to author, December 15, 1981.

E. Grady Bogue is chancellor of Louisiana State University in Shreveport. He has served on the staffs of both the Tennessee Higher Education Commission and Memphis State University, and was an American Council on Education Fellow in academic administration. He has long been active in the Association for Institutional Research.

Institutional researchers influence state government decisions through their information and analysis and their interpersonal skills.

Institutional Research and State Government — A State Agency View

Paul E. Lingenfelter

Institutional research plays an important role in state government because the products of institutional research—information and analysis—are central to decision making. In addition, institutional researchers as individuals often have direct or nearly direct contact with state agency staff on a number of technical and policy issues. Both the quality of the information and analysis they provide and the quality of their interpersonal relationships can influence decisions that are important to higher education.

The purpose of this chapter is to review the role of institutional research and the relationships between institutional researchers and state agencies from the perspective of state agency staff. State agencies are meant to include both agencies exclusively concerned with higher education (usually state coordinating agencies) and agencies in the executive and legislative branches of government that are involved in budgeting, regulation, and substantive legislation for higher education.

The discussion first considers the statutory and pragmatic roles and responsibilities of institutions, state higher education agencies, and legislative and executive agencies. This is followed by a brief analysis of the role of institutional research in the decision-making process and a few comments on approaches for achieving effective working relationships. Although many of these comments may apply to all sectors of higher education and to federal as well as state government, the primary focus is upon the relationships between public institutions and state governments.

Statutory and Pragmatic Perspectives on Roles and Responsibilities

The statutory and constitutional status of public colleges and universities varies among the states. In twenty-three states some form of constitutional recognition of higher education is made (Carnegie, 1976), but the specific powers granted to institutions are often vague or general. In most cases, the status of public institutions and, more importantly, the conditions and authority under which they operate are determined by statute. In addition, the largest single source of revenue for virtually all public institutions is tax revenues appropriated by the state legislature. Consequently, in both an explicit legal sense (in most states) and in an implicit political sense, the legislative and executive branches of state government exercise sovereignty over public colleges and universities.

Despite the explicit and implicit subordination of public institutions to the state, higher education institutions enjoy a somewhat privileged status in many states. Statutes often are written to provide operational flexibility to colleges and universities that is not granted to other state agencies, and elected or appointed governing boards usually exercise authority that is reserved for the governor or other elected officials in the case of other state organizations. This partial insulation of higher education institutions from the state has deep historical and philosophical roots in the traditions of American colleges and universities, even though its legal basis is much less firmly rooted.

From the perspective of state agency staff (particularly in the legislative and executive branches), a special status for higher education is more likely to be viewed as a questionable privilege than a right. While the partial insulation of higher education from the political process may be socially desirable, state agency staff struggling with conflicting demands in the political process are likely to be annoyed rather than persuaded by arguments about the rights and responsibilities of colleges and universities that would limit their access to information or their options in the decision-making process. From the state perspective, higher education is merely one of many social priorities.

This perspective and the proximity to elected decision makers sometimes can lead state agency staff to be aggressive, excessive, and unrelenting in the pursuit of information. Both philosophically and pragmatically, it is difficult for institutions to argue that such demands exceed the rights of state level staff. If agency staff demands are unduly burdensome, the most appropriate institutional response is usually to acknowledge their right to information, cooperate to the greatest possible extent, and work, without complaining, to communicate problems and costs of responding. Institutions can expect little relief from unreasonable demands for information so long as agency staff have reason to believe institutions are hiding something or are uncooperative as a matter of principle.

In general, debates over policy alternatives are likely to be most productive when they focus on concrete policy outcomes rather than the relative roles and responsibilities of the participants in the process. Despite these limitations, however, it may be useful in this discussion to make a few observations about various roles in the decision-making process. Both institutional representatives and state agency staff need to be sensitive to the perceptions others have of their role and to avoid rigid notions of their own responsibilities and prerogatives.

Institutional Responsibilities. Institutions are responsible for providing instructional, research, and public service programs that are effective, efficient, and relevant to public needs. Institutional representatives are expected to have a special interest in their programs, to advocate the need for resources, and to seek ways to enhance and expand the contribution of higher education to the public.

As institutional representatives articulate these interests, however, it is important that they remember and acknowledge higher education's subordination to the broader public interest. From this perspective, higher education's only "right" is to serve well. Institutional researchers are responsible for responding to requests for information openly, honestly, and in ways that contribute to well-informed decisions. This is not to suggest that a rational model of decision making can replace the give and take of the political process. The decisions made in the political process are likely to be better, however, if all participants have access to and can argue on the basis of good information.

It is also important for institutions to avoid seeking desirable administrative flexibility by arguing peripheral issues such as academic freedom. It is possible to preserve academic freedom within a complex and cumbersome bureaucratic framework just as it is possible to violate academic freedom in a laissez-faire regulatory environment.

Both institutions and state agencies should be sensitive to the operational consequences of regulations and requests for information. Desirable outcomes in these areas are more likely, however, if institutions cooperate and strive for effective communication rather than seek to be exempted from governmental "interference" in their activities. Terry Sanford, who has served as both a governor and university president, noted, "More universities have suffered from political indifference than have ever been upset by political interference" (Carnegie Foundation for the Advancement of Teaching, 1976, inside title page).

Responsibilities of State Higher Education Agencies. The specific role of the state higher education agency often depends upon its statutory responsibilities and the informal practices of the decision-making process. Some state agencies for higher education have governance responsibilities. They hire administrative staff, let contracts, and establish operating policies for the institutions in their jurisdiction. Other state agencies are limited to coordinating and budgeting functions, which may deal in important ways with major policy issues but stop short of administrative policies or a formal role in personnel matters. Other state agencies may play a strictly advisory role to the legislative and executive branches of government. In addition to statutory differences, the role of all such agencies in the decision-making process will vary to some extent according to traditions and their access to and credibility with legislative leadership and the executive branch.

All state higher education agencies, however, have a responsibility to contribute to the decision-making process by acting as a channel of communcation between higher education and government. By virtue of their function, state higher education agencies are natural advocates for the public services provided by colleges and universities. By virtue of their proximity to the governmental decision-making process, however, state agencies also have a responsibility to reflect the broader concerns of state government to higher education.

State higher education agencies cannot be effective if they are the intellectual or political captive of either higher education, state government as a whole, or some segment of state government. The most effective state agency should be responsive to different concerns from all of these perspectives and should work as a mediating agent to improve the quality of communication and the quality of decisions made in the political arena concerning higher education.

Implicit in this role is the need to maintain and improve the quality of information that is provided to legislative and executive decision makers. Higher education agencies should consider the development of cost-effective information systems a high priority. Institutions interested in avoiding burdensome reporting should encourage and support state agency efforts to build a solid system for providing the information used in the decision-making process. Such a system helps identify important policy issues and improves the credibility of both the agency and higher education in the political process.

Finally, state higher education agencies should be a means of focusing and unifying the interactions between the higher education community and state government. It is unrealistic, even in highly centralized higher education systems, to expect all communication with government to flow through a state agency. The interests of higher education are likely to be advanced, however, if a coherent, broadly based coalition of institutions works together rather than at cross-purposes in the political process. State higher education agencies are ideally placed to foster such a coalition. If for some reason the agency is incapable of serving that role, institutions should consider creating a similar, less formal mechanism.

Legislative and Executive Agency Responsibilities. Legislative and executive branch agencies also are structured in diverse ways. In some states legislative agencies are bipartisan and serve both houses of the legislature. In other states legislative staff are split along partisan lines and between houses of the legislature. As in the case of higher education agencies, however, the structural location of the agency is somewhat incidental to the substance of the agency role.

Legislative and executive branch agency staff are a major means through which elected officials acquire information and sift through policy alternatives. They also depend on staff to perform the technical work through which decisions are implemented. Staff naturally and appropriately see their first obligation to their employers, and they identify their own roles closely with the responsibilities and prerogatives of the elected officials they serve.

These responsibilities require legislative and executive agencies to be sensitive to the concerns of higher education, as it is both a constituent group and an important public policy area. Accordingly, these agencies have incentives to work effectively with college and university staff. In the context of their broader responsibilities, however, higher education is simply one among many public interest groups, all of which have some claim on limited resources. As participants in the decision-making process through which the needs of many interests must be weighed and somehow accommodated, legislative and executive staff are normally critical, skeptical analysts of various claims on state resources. Higher education representatives should expect and receive tough questions from all state agency staff, whether their role is limited to higher education or broader in scope.

In a philosophical sense, it is hard to exclude totally any area of public colleges and universities from the legitimate purview of state agency staff. The size of the public investment in higher education and its social importance are sufficient justification for state agency staff to be concerned with virtually everything that might impair or enhance an institution's effectiveness. As a practical matter, however, state agency staff need to focus on matters of broad concern, not the minutiae of institutional operations. State agencies cannot deal effectively with policy matters if they get too deeply involved in operational issues, and institutional administrators cannot function effectively if they are continually being second-guessed.

The lines between policy and operations, between coordination and governance, and between governance and administration will never be sharp and clear to people with different perspectives. Someone once observed that these differences are more like marble cake than layer cake; everybody agrees there are differences, but they are all mixed together. In view of the futility of drawing sharp role distinctions, the participants in the process should practice restraint in exercising their own roles and be sensitive to the roles others play.

To some extent the degree to which institutions can keep state agencies out of administrative matters depends upon the ability of both parties to deal effectively with policy issues. In some cases state agencies may intrude into management areas without apparent justification or provocation, but often such intrusions are made to achieve a policy objective. Institutions should try to respond to policy concerns in ways that minimize the likelihood of a state-imposed administrative or statutory solution. Likewise, state agencies should seek ways of achieving policy objectives that avoid cumbersome regulation or excessive bureaucratic involvement.

Institutional Research in the Decision-Making Process

State government decisions concerning higher education can be described in two broad categories, macro and micro. Macro decisions are those which periodically determine higher education's share of state resources and decide fundamental questions of governance, structure, or policy. Micro decisions are those which determine the allocation of resources within higher education and a variety of regulatory issues ranging from program coordination and approval to auditing and accounting procedures.

Both macro and micro governmental decisions are political in that they are directly or indirectly influenced by the consideration of various interests. Another distinction can be made, however, between low-visibility, *small p,* political decisions and *capital P* Political decisions, where partisan politics or conflict between other major coalitions (such as geographical regions) are important factors. Most decisions, even many macro decisions, are small p in that partisanship or regional interests are not major factors. Sometimes, however, decisions which normally might be routine, small p decisions become capital P decisions. A powerful elected official may decide that the importance of a particular issue to his or her constituents warrants a major expenditure of political capital. Or a number of peripheral, normally small p issues may be tied together in an effort to build a winning coalition on a major partisan or regional issue.

This distinction is useful in that the capital P decision-making process is usually less predictable and more difficult for higher education institutions to influence. Most higher education issues are small p decisions, and efforts to avoid the entanglement of these issues in the more volatile capital P process are well advised.

Occasionally, however, a higher education issue (such as proposed cuts in federal support for student aid) becomes an important capital P question. Information provided by institutional researchers has a role to play in such decisions, because decision makers use information in an effort to influence the public and other decision makers. Direct public contacts and capital P Political considerations, however, are probably more significant factors than information standing alone.

Macro Decision Making. Elected decision makers, particularly those in leadership positions, are more likely to become directly involved in the macro decisions that determine the total higher education budget or establish broad policies for higher education operations. At this level, resource allocation decisions are influenced in part by the perceived needs of higher education in comparison to other needs. Of course, budget decisions are also influenced by their effects on groups that provide political support. Because many in higher education tend not to become deeply involved in the political process, the effects of decisions upon political supporters is often not a strong consideration. Accordingly, information concerning needs may be more important than political support when macro decisions concerning higher education are being made. For the same reason, however, higher education may be at a disadvantage when competition for scarce resources is intense. Elected officials naturally tend to respond to their supporters when times are tough.

Institutional researchers have a responsibility to provide institutional leaders with information that documents the needs of higher education in terms that are clear and direct. To be most effective such information should be brief, simply presented, and focused on general concerns that justify additional resources or broad policy issues. Macro level fiscal concerns could include inadequate faculty compensation, increasing costs for utilities and other goods and services, enrollment increases or decreases, or a major effort to begin, expand, or strengthen an important academic program. In some states tuition rates are a highly visible, macro-level policy issue.

While materials attempting to influence macro decisions should be simple, direct, and compelling, this requirement should not be interpreted to mean that superficial, unsophisticated analysis is adequate. Legislative and executive agency staff are likely to dissect the information provided to decision makers. While good analysis will look even better after its underpinnings are examined, both higher education's case and its credibility will suffer if a staff analysis exposes sloppy or misleading work.

In addition to being clear and straightforward, information provided to decision makers should normally be a positive presentation of higher education's case, not a litany of past injustice nor an attack on competitors for state resources. Negative approaches subtly (or not so subtly) criticize decision makers' past judgments and question their ability to evaluate needs fairly. If the situation warrants some kind of negative analysis, it should be presented with great sensitivity.

Micro Decision Making. Elected political officials often choose to be less directly involved in decisions concerning the allocation of resources within higher education or the regulation of programs and operations. A decision-making system that involves legislative budget agency staff, coordinating or governing boards, and/or higher education institutions and interests often is given the responsibility for making most micro decisions.

This decision-making system is never granted autonomy from elected decision makers, however. It is used by elected officials to resolve conflicts internal to higher education and to make decisions that require technical expertise. The micro decision-making system is expected to be sensitive to local interests and the political and policy concerns of elected officials. In short, it is expected to work well enough to avoid swamping elected officials with unresolved internal conflicts and technical arguments. The micro decision-making system also can provide needed operating flexibility to institutions.

Some micro decisions must be formally ratified by elected officials, and the potential for legislative or executive involvement always exists. If the micro decision-making system does not resolve conflicts successfully, they are likely to become macro, or capital P issues. If the existing system fails to resolve large numbers of conflicts within higher education, elected officials are likely to modify or restructure it in order to control the nature and quantity of issues that require their direct attention.

As stated earlier the micro decision-making process involves legislative and executive staff, state agencies for higher education, institutions, and other higher education interests. The role of these different actors varies with the issue and the traditions of the state, but the importance of legislative and executive branch staff should be stressed.

It can be easy to underestimate the potential influence of staff when direct access to elected decision makers is available. Good staff members will not aggressively attempt to intrude personal views into the macro decision-making process nor will they knowingly create political problems for their employers. Elected officials, however, depend on staff to assure the effectiveness of the micro decision-making process, and they will defer to staff on many technical and sometimes not so technical matters. Good relationships with staff should be an important goal for institutions, state higher education agencies, and institutional researchers in both settings. As a wise and experienced friend counsels, "Staff can kill you."

The techniques used in the micro decision-making system to make budget decisions are as varied as the systems themselves. In some states a process of analyzing individual budget requests and discussing issues ("negotiating" to some) is used by the state agency, executive budget staff, and/or legislative staff to develop a plan for allocating resources within higher education. The plan is then submitted to elected officials for their consideration and action. In other states a participative process is used to develop a budget formula for allocating resources.

Budget formulas are attractive to some because of their mathematical precision, predictability, and "fairness." While they clearly can be a useful means of conflict resolution, there is no question that the negotiations needed to develop a formula also require compromise and the give and take of a political process.

To others, including this writer, the disadvantages of budget formulas outweigh their advantages. Their precision suggests an unreal degree of objectivity and rationality, and a rigid adherence to a formula over time can result in failure to adapt to changing conditions. The issues that formulas handle well (per student funding) can be managed as one of several important budget concerns. If the participants in the decision-making process can tolerate the ambiguities of a more flexible approach, they may avoid spending time on technical, formula approaches to issues that are more appropriately handled as matters of judgment and policy.

Institutions and institutional researchers clearly have an important role to play in the micro decision-making process and a high stake in its success. Because the micro decision-making system tends to be technically oriented, the quality of information provided is critically important. Institutional researchers should actively seek ways of improving the procedures used to collect data for decision making. Institutions might find some short-term advantage in manipulating data or being uncooperative, but both institutional flexibility and good relationships with elected decision makers depend upon the success of the micro decison-making system.

Achieving Effective Working Relationships

Human relationships are at the core of the political process, and effective working relationships depend upon the effort and wisdom that the people involved bring to the relationship. In a very real sense both institutions and state agency staff need to contribute to good relationships, and either party can make them difficult to achieve.

Institutional representatives may feel at a disadvantage in relationships with state government staff because they depend upon government for resources. In a strict sense, political power often is unevenly distributed in such relationships; if the more powerful individual is difficult to work with, life can be frustrating at best.

It is important to recognize, however, that no participant in the process has unlimited knowledge, power, or influence. Institutional researchers and other institutional representatives know more about the details of institutional operations than any other participant in the decision-making process. Legislative and executive agency staff are closer to those who have formal decision-making power, but even elected officials are constrained by cross pressures and the need to maintain their supporting coalitions. The staff of state higher education agencies benefit from their formal role in the process and their knowledge of higher education, but they rarely have formal decision-making authority and they cannot know all the intimate details of internal institutional operations.

While no participant in the process can ignore the need to establish effective relationships, the dependency of higher education on governmental support makes the development of good working relationships especially critical to institutional researchers. At the risk of belaboring the obvious, the following list suggests ways that institutional researchers can contribute to better relationships with state agency staff:

1. *Meet deadlines.* Government schedules are often tight and rigid. Late submissions can force harried state agency staff to miss deadlines or compress work into too short a time period. Thus, late submissions generate ill will and contribute to errors or misunderstandings.

2. *Pay attention to detail.* The appropriations and legislative process demands precision. State agency staff are accustomed to expecting precision, even when it may not be absolutely necessary in certain supporting documents. Technical errors, arithmetic errors, and so on, suggest sloppy work or disrespect for the decision-making process. Technical errors are also likely to generate requests for additional information.

3. *Avoid moral superiority complexes.* People who have an analytical orientation are sometimes offended by the marketplace aspects of the political process. It is important to understand that the political process is designed to decide a large number of complex issues in a short period of time through competition for votes among differing viewpoints. As a marketplace of power and influence, the political process has a rationality of its own that warrants respect, even when it seems to run counter to individual ideas of sensible or proper decision making.

4. *Avoid intellectual superiority complexes.* Higher education staff should know more about the intricate details of higher education than governmental staff, and to the extent necessary, they should attempt to communicate this special knowledge. They should not try to educate state agency staff. This difference is subtle, but important.

5. *Avoid analytical games, tricks, sleight of hand, or even "innocently" misleading presentations of data.* Any possible gains from such techniques are likely to be far less than the losses in credibility. Such tactics insult the intelligence of governmental staff and generate ill will and mistrust

at best. At worst they will generate excessive requests for information and sanctions.

6. *Try to be sensitive to the challenges and problems others face.* People listen better if their concerns are also being heard.

7. *Keep it simple.* Some policy-oriented institutional research uses sophisticated techniques that are virtually incomprehensible to those unfamiliar with the profession's esoterica. If the point cannot be made simply and powerfully, it is hardly worth trying to make it. Complex concepts should be expressed in clear language. Professional jargon can be an implicit put-down, and it is offensive to many in the political decision-making process.

8. *Avoid defensiveness.* It is fine to accentuate the positive and it is smart to try to control the agenda, but occasionally conceding a point shows respect for others and an awareness that all truth and justice is not on one side of the issue.

9. *Avoid questioning the pertinence or motives of an inquiry.* If requested information seems likely to mislead or be of little use, a sensitive discussion of the questioner's concerns or an offer of additional, related information may be well received and helpful. However, aggressive questions (Why do you want to know? What are you planning to do with this?) may insult the questioner's competence, intrude inappropriately into his or her work, or suggest the institution has something to hide.

10. *If a caveat is needed in response to a question, make it simple and clear.* Do not provide voluminous supporting detail or other information that has not been requested. At best extra information can irritate; at worst it can generate further requests.

11. *Seek ways to achieve mutual benefit.* If reporting requirements are burdensome or misguided, relationships may be improved by suggesting ways to provide what is needed more effectively and efficiently. If such suggestions are not sensitive to the needs of state agency staff, however, they can be misunderstood.

12. *Work to improve the quality of analysis in the presentation of higher education's case in the decision-making process.* Solid work wins respect and support among state agency staff and helps to build credibility.

Faithful adherence to all of the above cannot change the fundamental dynamics of the political process, make all relationships smooth and satisfying, nor guarantee success for the interest of higher education. These suggestions, however, may help avoid unnecessary and unproductive static in the political process. In addition, they may contribute to understanding and better communication between institutions and state governmental agencies.

Reference

Carnegie Foundation for the Advancement of Teaching. *The States and Higher Education.* San Francisco: Jossey-Bass, 1976.

Paul E. Lingenfelter is deputy director of fiscal affairs for the Illinois Board of Higher Education. He previously worked at the University of Michigan. He has done research on the higher education budgeting process in several Midwestern states and has contributed to several Jossey-Bass volumes.

Federal educational statistical activities and federal support of research about higher education in general and about institutional operations in particular are primary activities that assist institutional research.

Institutional Research, Politics, and the Federal Government

John Folger

The federal government has been a major influence on the development of higher education since World War II, and has been the primary supporter of academic research, of the expansion of selected areas such as education for the health professions, and of student aid. More than 300 different federal programs have an effect on higher education, and most of them were established in the last twenty-five years.

The political history of the federal role has been an interesting one too, because most federal initiatives were justified indirectly, as necessary for veterans' readjustment (the GI Bill), national defense (the National Defense Education Act), health (Health Professions Education Assistance Act), or other national objectives. Because there is no mention of education in the Constitution, it is one of the powers and functions reserved to the states, and there has been a presumption on the part of many congressmen that the federal government should only intervene in education when there is some other national purpose that has to be met that requires the participation of the colleges.

The growth, definition, and redefinition of the federal role has been chronicled very well, both in descriptive terms (how big, and what programs) and in terms of the political dynamics involved (who supported what, and why). Good accounts of the process have been provided by Lawrence Gladieaux and Thomas Wolanin (1976), Chester Finn, Jr. (1978), the Advisory Commission on Intergovernmental Relations (1981), the Institute for Educational Leadership (1976), Aims McGuiness (1981), and Sproull, Weiner, and Wolf (1978).

Rather than recapitulate the whole history and current status of the relations between institutions and the federal government, this chapter focuses on the role of federal programs in supporting institutional research, broadly defined. Federal educational statistical activities and federal support of research about higher education in general and about institutional operations in particular are primary activities that assist institutional research.

Institutional research is defined broadly to include those studies, policy analyses, and information collections that assist college administrators to understand and deal with both the internal operations and external environment of their institution. This includes studies about public opinion, fiscal and demographic trends, student career choice processes, and college choices of students, as well as studies of curriculum, teaching effectiveness, and other internal operations of the institution. Studies done by the business office, admissions office, or other units of the institution are included in the scope of federal-institutional relations that will be examined.

Federal Statistics and Institutional Research

The first function of the Bureau of Education, established after the Civil War, was to collect statistics and prepare an annual report about education, and for its first fifty or sixty years the bureau (later the Office of Education) did very little else except report about education. Collection of statistics and preparation of reports about education did not lead to a more active federal role in higher education. The first Land Grant College Act was passed in 1862 (just prior to the time the Bureau of Education was established) and there were a few other federal initiatives in the next fifty years: the Hatch Act of 1887 for agricultural research, the Second Land Grant Act of 1890, and the Smith-Lever Act of 1914 for agricultural and home economics vocational education, for example. It was World War II, however, that led to major new federal initiatives in aid to higher education: the GI Bill in 1944, the support of basic research (the National Science Foundation, 1950), and a major expansion during the 1950s of defense and health-related research being done in colleges and universities.

The original purpose of federal statistical collections was to provide national information about education. The value of federal statistical data for institutional management and operations was quite limited. Data were reported on a few items like enrollment and finance, but until the postwar period, very little attention was paid to standard definitions, timely reporting, or meeting the information needs of institutions.

Higher education was not a public policy issue of any importance prior to World War II at either the federal or state level. Few students were involved, few dollars were involved, and most of those dollars came from the private sector. As late as 1940 three fourths of the funds for higher education came from tuition, private gifts, and endowment, and only one fourth from federal, state, and local tax sources. By 1950 tax revenues (federal, state, and local) were over half of all revenue for higher education and by 1980 they were over 60 percent (Advisory Commission on Intergovernmental Relations, 1981, Tables 1 and 3).

The expansion of the federal role in education led to an expansion of statistics about the new programs in education. Information was collected and reported about research activity (by the National Science Foundation) and about the many new programs that developed during the 1950s, 1960s, and 1970s. Regulatory functions of the federal government in civil rights enforcement for minorities and women and the enforcement of the rights of the handicapped generated a large volume of reports. Institutions began to complain about the paperwork burden and the costs of compliance with federal mandates (Shulman, 1979).

The massive increases in regulatory reporting had little connection with the general purpose statistics, although information about enrollment by race was added to the collection job of the National Center for Education Statistics (NCES). Estimates are that general purpose statistics collected by NCES were less than 10 percent of the total respondent burden upon colleges and universities (staff estimates provided to the Advisory Committee on Educational Statistics).

The pressure to cut back on all reporting has made it very difficult to add any new features or questions to the Higher Education General Information Survey, the primary instrument for collecting general purpose statistics from colleges and universities.

Even if NCES had had the resources to expand their data collection to provide more information for institutions, and even if there had been a demand from the institutions to provide the data, it is doubtful that the center would have gotten clearance to collect the data, because the pressures to reduce the paperwork burden were so strong.

A congressional mandate would lead to approval of new data

collection, but interests of the users might not be compelling. The effects of both the budget and the efforts to cut back on federal paperwork constrained the collection of statistics about higher education in the late 1970s. There were a few congressionally mandated expansions—vocational education and data about minority enrollment—but the collection of other statistics either remained the same or was cut back.

General purpose statistics (information about enrollments, institutional characteristics, finances, facilities, and programs) changed slowly. The priority for general purpose statistics seemed to slip a little in the 1970s as Congress and the executive branch pressed for information about special topics.

As Congress and the executive branch began to expand programs, there were pressures to supply more and better data to evaluate or to justify programs. However, frequent delays in supplying statistics and relevant information led the critics to attack the adequacy of the whole program. In the mid-1950s the secretary of HEW, Marion Folsom, had the first of several reviews of education statistics made by outside groups. It was headed by Helen Walker, a statistician from Columbia University. Three or four years later a second outside review was headed by Gertrude Cox, director of the Institute of Statistics at North Carolina State University. These evaluations showed that as compared with labor statistics, health statistics, or population statistics, education statistics had a low budget. The staff was less professionalized and much smaller and had relatively poor information about the accuracy of the statistics they had collected. The Office of Education, furthermore, was not collecting and reporting their statistics soon enough to be useful to administrators at either the federal or institutional level. Despite these criticisms, the Office of Education moved very slowly to make any changes.

The first priority of the Office of Education leadership centered on the many new programs they had to administer. Since Congress only put sporadic and occasional pressure on for the improvement of educational statistics, the Office of Education's response was slow. Institutions of higher education and state departments of education also only exerted occasional pressure on the Office of Education about statistical programs because they too were much more interested in new programs that were being developed to help college construction, expand vocational education, provide graduate fellowships, and other good things.

The Association of Collegiate Registrars, and the National Association of College Business Officers were active in suggesting improvements to the statistical programs, particularly in the use of standard definitions, but the center of attention of the more influential associations of institutional chief executives, such as the American Council on Education, the Land Grant College Association, and the Association of American Universities, was directed to the larger and more important (to the institutions) new support programs such as the National Defense Education Act (1958), the Higher Education Facilities Act (1963), the Arts and Humanities Foundation (1965), and the programs of the Higher Education Act (1965).

Educational statistics were something that everyone complained about (slowness, lack of data about current policy issues, and so on), but institutional and association leaders were generally too busy with other federal issues to do much about it. Education statistics were a second priority in the Office of Education and with the influential interest groups.

Not only were education statistics a second priority among educators, they were a second priority among statisticians, too. The statistical leadership in the federal government was located in other, larger and more professional, agencies, like the Census Bureau, the Bureau of Labor Statistics, and the Bureau of the Budget. The Office of Education had a difficult time in recruiting and retaining top statistical talent. Alexander Mood, a nationally known statistician, headed the statistical work of the office for a while, but low salaries and limited opportunities to do either analytic or methodological work that would advance statistical careers made it difficult to attract top professionals to the staff of the agency. There were several periods when the agency had only an acting leader, which provided additional complications in improving the program.

In an effort to give more priority to education statistics, the statistical function was reorganized within the Education Division. The NCES was given a statutory basis in the Educational Amendments of 1974 (National Center for Education Statistics, 1976). It, along with the National Institute of Education (NIE), was a part of the Office of the Assistant Secretary for Education. NCES was not responsible for collection of program statistics for the various education activities but instead was expected to collect and report general purpose statistics and develop statistical information about important education policy issues. NCES was also directed by Congress to prepare an annual report on the condition of education in the nation as a means of providing current data for congressmen, federal officials, educational leaders, and the general public about the major issues in education.

NCES has done a good job of reporting on the national condition of education, incorporating data from a variety of sources, including the Census Bureau and a number of research studies, as well as their own statistics to report on a variety of current educational policy issues. NCES has also had to respond to a number of congressional mandates for data collection, including such diverse topics as safe schools and vocational education outcomes.

As a result of the new mandates and a budget that has not expanded proportionately, the NCES program has given very little emphasis to the needs of institutions and states for data because they have put nearly all of their attention on the needs of the federal government.

The needs of institutional researchers for statistics include national figures but they also include state data, statistics for peer institutions, and special analyses of issues that may be of more concern to institutions than to the federal government. Institution-specific statistics are less available today than they were two decades ago, unless an institution wants to purchase tapes and develop its own analysis.

NCES necessarily puts top priority on the needs of the federal government, particularly the provision of data for policy questions that are important to Congress. It puts second priority on general purpose national statistics, and third priority on state and institutional statistics.

These differences in priorities have come to a head in the last few months, with the Office of Management and Budget (OMB) directing NCES to eliminate some surveys that have been a part of the national statistics collected in the Higher Education General Information Survey for a number of years. OMB is arguing that there is no federal need for this data, and that NCES should not burden institutional respondents to supply it unless there is a federal requirement for it. NCES is maintaining that there is a national need for the data for state and institutional users, as well as national users, and that it should be collected.

At issue is the federal role in educational statistics and how that should be defined. Should NCES be limited to collecting data only for federal programs in education or should it collect national statistics about the size, cost, and operation of higher education? There is a need for this information and for national information about a number of policy questions that are important to states and institutions, whether the federal government is doing anything about them or not.

Institutional leaders are even more concerned about other cuts in federal programs, so it is not clear how much attention and political pressure can be brought to bear on the statistical cutbacks.

In the past eight to ten years the Office of Education and NCES have devoted very little effort to trying to cultivate the client groups at the state or institutional level that could assist in supporting their statistical functions with Congress or OMB. As mentioned above, NCES has concentrated so much on federal needs that they have been able to provide very little new information for the state and institutional constituencies. In the 1980s high quality statistics that are of value to institutional research may be less available than they have been in the past decade, and the relatively low priority for educational statistics will probably make this a difficult situation to change.

This assessment is unfortunate, because the development of high-quality statistics about education in the country is uniquely a federal role, and one that neither states nor institutions can be expected to perform efficiently or well. The federal government should do the job, but the political environment does not give much cause for optimism.

Research About Higher Education

There are few activities that are as large and important as higher education that do so little research about themselves. It is estimated that higher education institutions spent over $70 billion in fiscal year 1982, but there is less than 0.5 percent of the education budget spent on research and analysis designed to make the enterprise operate more effectively. Expenditures for education research are less than 2 percent of federal research expenditures.

The federal role has been crucial in the support of research in nationally important areas. They have supported a majority of the basic research and a large part of the applied research in areas such as agriculture, health, national defense, and space exploration. But federal contributions to research about education at either the elementary and secondary level or the higher education level have been relatively small.

While the Office of Education conducted occasional studies of educational issues during its data-collecting era before World War II, systematic support of research began after 1950. In 1954 Congress passed the Cooperative Research Act which authorized the Office of Education to make grants to colleges, universities, and state departments of education for research on topics of national interest (Advisory Commission on Intergovernmental Relations, 1981). The cooperative research program was designed to prevent the buildup of an in-house staff; the research was contracted out to colleges and education agencies. The program was initially funded in 1956 with $1 million and made small grants primarily to individual researchers (Sproull, Weiner, and Wolf, 1978).

Cooperative research expanded from $1 million in fiscal year 1957 to $11.5 million in fiscal year 1964 (Sproull, Weiner, and Wolf, 1978). The primary interest of the leadership in both Congress and the Office of Education, however, was not a program of grants to individuals to do basic studies about education but an interest in applied studies that dealt with important national issues.

These studies were sometimes the outgrowth of legislation rather than the basis for it. The Coleman study of desegregation, for example, followed the passage of the 1964 Civil Rights Act, while the National Commission on Financing Postsecondary Education followed the Higher Education Amendments of 1972, when the issue of federal institutional support had been extensively debated.

The growing dissatisfaction within HEW with the results of the many independent studies being made by the cooperative research program led to recommendations for much more sharply focused research centers. The first of these was established in 1964. This was followed in 1965 by the establishment of twenty regional laboratories that were independent, were federally funded, emphasized focused research, and were also responsible for dissemination. The laboratory program was authorized in the Elementary and Secondary Education Act of 1965, along with the ERIC dissemination system, and from their inception most of the centers and laboratories emphasized elementary and secondary issues.

Exceptions included a center for the study of higher education, which operated for about a decade at the University of California, Berkeley, a national center for higher education management systems at the Western Interstate Commission on Higher Education, and a center of vocational education at Ohio State University. Subsequently, one of the laboratories (in North Carolina) emphasized higher education issues but it was phased out after only a few years of operation. Some of the other laboratories and centers occasionally did studies that were relevant to institutional research interests.

The laboratories and centers were designed to provide an applied focus and to disseminate research to practitioners. From their inception they were subject to repeated criticism, program reviews, and management audits. The staff in the Office of Education that was responsible for managing the program had a very high rate of turnover and the program staff were overloaded with monitoring responsibilities. The program never developed any stability of management or direction. In a nine-year period there were eight directors of the Bureau of Research in the Office of Education (Sproull, Weiner, and Wolf, 1978).

Expenditures for research in the Office of Education jumped from less than $14 million in fiscal year 1963 to about $100 million in fiscal year 1966 as a result of the establishment of the laboratories, centers, and a program of research in vocational education and education of the handicapped. From that point to the start of the National Institute of Education (NIE) in 1972, the funding for research did not follow any consistent pattern of growth, and in fiscal year 1972 funds for research in education were less than $125 million.

The establishment of the mission-oriented laboratories and centers did not reduce the congressional criticism of the Office of Education research program. The program had weak administration, too much was expected from it too soon, and congressional critics got lots of ammunition from frequent administrative foul-ups. The Office of Education expanded the program too fast, without carefully thought-out plans and with considerable differences of opinion about goals and purposes of the total research effort.

By 1970, in a search for a more manageable, or better-managed, research effort, the administration proposed a new agency, the NIE, that would be separate from the program operations in the Office of Education and would bring together the various research support activities in the office into a single agency. A good account of the origins and early development of NIE is contained in Sproull, Weiner, and Wolf (1978).

NIE was formed by bringing in most of the research programs in the Office of Education with their existing budgets. It began with a $110 million budget, and in terms of overall support, has gone downhill ever since. The NIE budget for fiscal year 1982, is about one fourth the level of support in 1972 in constant dollars.

Most of the research, development, and dissemination that NIE inherited from the Office of Education dealt with educational issues and problems of elementary and secondary education; only about 5 to 10 percent of the support was for research, development, or dissemination at the higher education level. The emphasis has not shifted appreciably in the intervening decade, partly because the funding of NIE has gone down in constant dollar terms in most of the years since then. NIE has had several plans to expand work on higher education problems, but the plans were generally aborted because every year the agency's funding either did not get increased or got cut.

The influential educational interest groups have only occasionally been mobilized in the support of educational research, and the constituent groups who are strongly interested (the educational researchers themselves) have not been influential enough to get support stabilized and maintained or increased. Policy leaders in the federal government in both Congress and the executive branch have been quite skeptical about the value of educational research. Their view is that it does not provide enough practical answers and does not lead to much educational improvement. Other critics believe that educational research is not sufficiently rigorous in theory or method to build a body of tested propositions that can be applied.

The federal government is the logical level of government to support research on education, particularly basic research and applied research on broad national issues. Individual colleges and universities and individual states cannot be expected to finance research on the major national trends that affect not only their campus and students, but all others. If the federal government does not support research, it probably will not get much support.

After more than a quarter of a century of support of educational research, the federal government shows no signs of developing a stable and predictable pattern of support. The relatively successful patterns of research administration that have been developed in basic science, agriculture, and health have not been transferred to education. As a result, the future of federal support of research in education appears quite uncertain, despite the obvious need to increase our understanding of ways to improve the operation of higher education institutions.

Other areas where federal support of research has flourished for a long time have had well-organized groups outside the government who have supported and influenced the growth of research in their field of interest, but the interest groups in support of education research have been fragmented, and have often worked at cross-purposes to each other. Some of the more influential groups, such as college presidents, chief state school officers, and local superintendents, frequently have higher priorities than the support of education research.

The current interest in, and increased priority for, quality improvement in education at all levels could provide a renewed interest in, and support for, research on a range of quality-improvement issues. If college and university leaders believe that research can actually improve their operations and get behind increased expenditures for research, it may be one of the few areas of federal support where increases are possible. But if the priority for research among the key constituent groups remains at the same level where it has been for the past decade, prospects for more research support will probably be poor.

References

Advisory Commission on Intergovernmental Relations. *The Federal Role in the Federal System: The Dynamics of Growth.* Washington, D.C.: Advisory Commission on Intergovernmental Relations, 1981. (A-82)
Finn, C. E., Jr. *Scholars, Dollars, and Bureaucrats.* Washington, D.C.: Brookings Institute, 1978.
Gladieaux, L., and Wolanin, T. *Congress and the Colleges.* Lexington, Mass.: Heath, 1976.
Institute for Educational Leadership. *Federalism at the Cross Roads.* Washington, D.C.: Institute for Educational Leadership, George Washington University, 1976.
McGuiness, A. "The Federal Government and Postsecondary Education." In P. Altbach and R. Berdahl (Eds.), *Higher Education in American Society.* Buffalo, N.Y.: Prometheus Books, 1981.
National Center for Education Statistics. *The Condition of Education 1976 Edition.* Washington, D.C.: U.S. Government Printing Office, 1976.
Shulman, C. H. *Compliance with Federal Regulations: At What Cost?* AAHE/ERIC Higher Education Research Report No. 6. Washington, D.C.: American Association for Higher Education, 1979.
Sproull, L., Weiner, S., and Wolf, D. *Organizing an Anarchy.* Chicago: University of Chicago Press, 1978.

John Folger is professor and codirector of the Center for Education Policy, Vanderbilt Institute for Public Policy Studies. He was associate director for policy at the Education Commission of the States, executive director of the Tennessee Higher Education, dean of the Graduate School and director of research at Florida State University, research associate and associate director of the Southern Regional Education Board. He is the author of two books and numerous articles on education, manpower, and human resource development.

Institutional researchers must *be in the institutional planning process in the coming years if institutional research is to remain a viable administrative specialty.*

The Future of Institutional Research

William F. Lasher
James W. Firnberg

The purposes of this chapter are to summarize and synthesize the work of the various chapter authors, to put into perspective the role of institutional research in higher education today, and to chart a course for its future role. As used throughout this text, the word politics should not conjure up in the mind of the reader the image of Boss Tweed, fiery political speeches of the likes of Clarence Darrow or William Jennings Bryan, nor smoke-filled caucus rooms. Instead, one should view politics in its purest sense as the influence individuals, organizations, or other entities have upon policy setting and decision making.

Nearly twenty years ago in their classic, *The Managerial Revolution in Higher Education,* Francis Rourke and Glenn Brooks (1966, p. 44) stated that institutional research was "at the heart of the trend toward the use of modern management techniques in higher education." However, institutional researchers themselves have disagreed about whether this trend should occur or not. There has long been an argument about whether institutional research should be oriented toward the theoretical study of higher education or be associated with administration, providing support to policy and decisionmaking. The more traditional view, taken by Nevitt Sanford, an early scholar in higher education, argues that institutional research should focus on academic and instructional issues. This approach emphasizes theoretical studies of the internal dynamics of colleges and universities, the effectiveness of an institution's academic program, and even the impact of higher education on students. On the other hand, John Dale Russell, who is acknowledged as one of the original institutional researchers, stressed that institutional research should focus more on administrative analysis, which supports decisions concerning institutional policy and planning.

The Russell model has, in recent years at least, been the predominant one. In many institutions, studies of educational effectiveness are left to educational psychologists, learning theorists, and other interested scholars. More general analyses of higher education organizations and their environments are left to faculty members in academic departments and/or research centers for the study of higher education.

The thesis of this sourcebook is based on the notion that this emphasis on administrative analysis—the Russell model—is appropriate for institutional research. Institutional research professionals should spend their time in support of decision making, policy making, and planning. However, as soon as one accepts this notion, one is forced—by the very nature of decision making, policy making, and planning—to deal with the political nature of institutions, of institutional research, and of information.

The primary activity of institutional researchers should be transforming data into information. The chapters by William L. Tetlow and Cameron L. Fincher deal with this fundamental activity and its consequences. Both speak of the nature of data and its relationship to information. As Fincher states, data are "the specific facts and details that are recorded in the routine operations of institutions' (Chapter 2, this volume). They result from observation or measurement. They are the building blocks of information. Data become information when they are selected, organized, or manipulated through analysis, and put into a form that is useful in some way to the user.

Data in their raw form are probably apolitical but they are not very useful either. However, as soon as they are acted upon, that is, selected, organized, and analyzed, they become politicized in two ways. First, as Tetlow mentions,"the very process of selection and organization of data involve many human judgments on the part of the information specialist" (Chapter 1, this volume). In other words, the very analysis that institutional researchers perform is itself a political act. His or her understanding of the intended use of the information, personal beliefs concerning the issue under consideration, and outlook for the institution are just three examples of areas that could render judgments that could affect the analysis and perhaps ultimately the decision.

Second, and related, information is always subject to more than one interpretation. That is, the institutional researcher generates and interprets the information within his or her frame of reference, and the user then receives it and uses it within his or her frame of reference. But that does not mean other individuals may not subsequently use the same information based on their own viewpoints. This subsequent use does not necessarily constitute misuse of the information, but it can.

These two outcomes of the transformation of data into information may explain why many institutional researchers prefer simply to transmit data and abstain from analyzing or interpreting them. In doing so, they do perform a function but they are not sufficiently involved in institutional policy making and planning.

Institutional researchers have traditionally assumed that their studies and analyses will be used as part of a rational decision process, in which all decision alternatives are fully explored and thoroughly analyzed before the final decision is made. Most experienced institutional researchers can probably recall many periods of frustration because the rational model was not followed, and their information was not used. Both Tetlow and Laura E. Saunders discuss this incongruity between the typical institutional researcher's view of decision making and the decision maker's actual behavior.

Saunders suggests that institutional researchers must understand the political setting of their institutions in order for their work to be used, and therefore have influence. In order for an institutional research office to become more effective, she suggests that four institutional characteristics be examined:

1. *The style of administration.* This is the dominant governance or administrative style, which depends on institutional evolution, external environment, leadership, and mission. Cohen and March's (1974) eight characterizations of administrative style are used to provide examples of different institutional research activities in different settings.

2. *The historical role of the institutional research office.* How is the institutional research office perceived on campus and what has been the nature of its work in the past?

3. *Relevant decision structures.* What are the processes by which different types of decisions are made? This includes both formal and informal processes.

4. *Key actors.* What individuals, groups, or bodies are involved in different types of decisions? Again, this includes both formal and informal involvement.

Once these four areas have been analyzed, Saunders then suggests that a full assessment of the strengths and weakness of the institutional research office be carried out. Changes in the role of the office can then be made or proposed.

Tetlow, on the other hand, suggests that the traditional institutional research assumption that decision making is rational lies in its historical development. Although it can be argued that institutional research began much earlier, the strong belief in the scientific method was the basis for many surveys done on higher education in the early twentieth century. Nevertheless, institutional research, as we know it today, grew out of the tremendous enrollment growth and infusion of federal research dollars after World War II. Because of these two phenomena, college and university officials felt they no longer had control over, nor understood completely, what was happening on their campuses. Administrators of the time called upon institutional researchers, by whatever name, to provide data to help understand and predict enrollments, budgets, class sizes, and so on.

In addition, the notion of self-study began about this time, and many of the studies launched were immediately confronted by the lack or inadequacy of available data. As a result, institutional researchers became rather adept at developing new or improving existing information systems. Later, many institutions developed more advanced analytical techniques involving operations research, modeling, and simulation techniques. All of this paralleled the development of rational analytical and decision-making techniques in government and business as well.

However, Tetlow goes on to argue that other views of the decision-making process now need to be considered. Paralleling Saunders, he suggests five schools of thought concerning how decisions are made, and how decision makers operate. He then argues that institutional researchers need to be able to adapt their activities to the situational context of the decision, the personality and style of the decision maker, and the intended use of the information which they provide.

Interestingly, Fincher gives a slightly different, more politicized interpretation of the history of institutional research.

Institutional research, management information, and institutional planning and development are the products of political pressures brought to bear upon institutions of higher education in an unprecedented period of growth and expansion. As colleges and universities became more dependent upon federal funding, there was an increased demand for uniform reporting systems that federal agencies could use in their documentation of societal demands and expectations for education beyond the high school. As higher education within the separate states became contralized with statewide governing and coordinating boards, state agencies placed a heavier burden upon institutions for enrollment, financial, and facilities data. As the public became suspicious that all was not well in the nation's efforts to provide mass education at the college level, private foundations, public commissions, and national councils accelerated their plea that institutions become more rational and analytical in their planning, management, and development (Chapter 2, this volume).

Actually the role of government, both federal and state, has had a greater influence on the development of institutional research than most professionals in the field are willing to admit. Instead they tend to see this role as an intrusion, which prevents them from doing what they "should" be doing.

John Folger describes the history of the federal role in both the development of statistics on higher education and research about higher education. The prospects for the future in either area are not optimistic. In the latter area, support for higher educational research over the last twenty-five years has not had the support, nor developed the following necessary to suggest a bright future. Many suspect the rigor of this kind of research and the practicality of its outcomes.

In the former area, Folger chronicles the increasing demand for data as the federal role in education expanded after World War II. However, he points out that it was the increases in regulatory reporting (that is, reports on research activity, civil rights enforcement, rights of the handicapped, and so on) rather than general purpose reporting (that is, the Higher Education General Information Survey) that caused institutions to begin to complain about the paperwork burden. Many institutional researchers have become mired in the ever-increasing demand for data that measure, or at least purport to measure, compliance with federal regulations. The complaints about the paperwork burden have had some impact, but at a cost of some of the more general data as well. Folger reports that institution-specific statistics are less available now than they have been in the past—unless the raw data themselves are purchased for subsequent analysis. But it is unlikely that the National Center for Education Statistics will provide the national, state, peer group, or institutional data in a form that is readily accessible and readily useable by institutions. Their priorities tend more toward federal needs. So it appears that while the compliance reporting continues, perhaps at a slightly lower level, institutional researchers will continue to find it difficult, but not impossible, to obtain some of the more general data they need to perform their jobs effectively at home.

In public institutions the role of state government probably affects institutional researchers more on a day-to-day basis than does the federal government. The increasing involvement and interest on the part of state governments in the coordination of higher education over the last two decades has been widely discussed in the literature. However, there seems to be no specific model of higher education coordination and control in the various states. Some state agencies have governance control. Others are limited to coordinating and budget functions and may affect institutional policy but not internal administrative practices. Still others are strictly advisory. Most importantly, the precise role and powers of state agencies are constantly evolving in the various states at their own rates. However, they all act as a communication channel between the institutions and state government. In this role, they have asked in varying degrees for data and information from institutions.

The amount of data requested by state agencies and their use are of political concern to institutions and to the institutional researchers involved in their preparation. The amount has probably increased more on a proportional basis than the increase in federal demands. As in all cases, the use of institutional information cannot be controlled by the institution once a request has been filed. Nevertheless, because the products of the institutional researchers' labors are used, in one way or another, in a state's decision making concerning higher education, institutional researchers are involved in the political affairs of their institution and have at least some influence on state decisions.

This being the case, the immediate issue then is what is the precise nature of the relationship between institutional researchers and state agency staff members. Both E. Grady Bogue and Paul E. Lingenfelter discuss this issue—Bogue, from the point of view of the institution, and Lingenfelter, from the point of view of a state agency staff member.

Lingenfelter offers two distinctions that are helpful in understanding this relationship. What he calls "macro" decisions concern higher education's share of state resources and fundamental questions of governance or policy. These are contrasted with "micro" decisions which involve the allocation of resources to institutions, and other regulatory issues concerning such things as program coordination or accounting procedures. All of these issues have political ramifications, but mostly, they are not very visible and do not become battlegrounds where great quantities of political capital are expended. Lingenfelter terms these issues "small p" political decisions. However, if they become major issues involving regional interests or other political coalitions willing to spend that political capital, he terms them *capital P* political decisions. Institutional researchers tend to work mostly on *micro/small p* issues, such as funding formulas, where their technical expertise and detailed knowledge of their institutions are most useful. They tend to be involved less in macro decisions, such as competing against the highway lobby, which have a greater probability of becoming *capital P* political issues. This does not mean the institutional researcher's political influence is unimportant. It is just normally not very visible.

Even though they approach the question from different frames of reference, Bogue and Lingenfelter basically agree on the best ways to foster an effective relationship between institutional researchers and state agency staff. They suggest that institutional researchers be honest and candid in their dealings with state agency staff, that they avoid deception or analytical gamesmanship, and that they avoid the we/them syndrome, that is, a condescending attitude. The goal should be mutual respect and trust, as in any human relationship. It is also important "to get to know each other," and be sensitive to the problems faced by state agency staff. In many ways, their work is institutional research too—just at a different level and on a different scale. In many cases, their backgrounds and talents are not that dissimilar from campus-based institutional researchers.

One of the natural uses of data collected nationally, at the state level, or by institutions is interinstitutional comparison. Undoubtedly this use stems from the explosion of data and information over the past several years and from the trend toward data-oriented management. However, institutional comparisons are as basic as the old question, How do we compare with X? The issue may be faculty salaries, enrollment increases, or sabbatical policies, just to name a few, but the interest is always there.

As a result, information exchange almost always occupies at least part of an institutional researcher's time. But what is to prevent a legitimate request for information from one institution being viewed in the same light as a data request from the state higher education agency or the federal government? Obviously there are political sensitivities that must be taken into account in this institutional research activity as with the other facets of the profession described previously. In addition, the issue of information use/misuse is especially relevant in this situation. Institutions do not take kindly to seeing in the media a comparison that shows them in a negative light when they understood the information was being exchanged for other purposes.

Deborah J. Teeter discusses these sensitivities and the nature of data exchanges in her chapter "The Politics of Comparing Data with Other Institutions." She indicates that even though exchange information can be used in making resource allocations, assessing productivity, and evaluating programs, institutions may be reluctant to participate. This reluctance usually hinges on "the purpose of the exchange, the complexity of the data involved, the effort required to participate, and the frequency with which responses are requested" (Chapter 4, this volume). Institutions need to see a relevant benefit for themselves from participating in such an activity. They will also be more willing to participate if the requirements of the exchange can be met with data and information that are readily available. For example, if great amounts of computer programming are required to provide the requested data in the right format, the level of interest on the part of the institution receiving the request may be quite low unless the issue under consideration is very important to them.

Nevertheless, one of the most important things to be gained from participation in information exchanges is the help such an activity provides in the development of an informal information network for each institutional researcher. This is an important weapon in the productive institutional researcher's arsenal. The ability to tap a network of knowledgeable, trusted colleagues for high-quality information and advice can make the institutional research professional a valued institutional asset.

The Future

At this point we should ask the question, "Has institutional research had a major impact on higher education?" Several years ago,

Lewis B. Mayhew (1966, p. 1) said, "Institutional research, although now well regarded, becoming affluent, and well supplied with technical devices, has yet to make a major impact on the main course of thinking about higher education. Are these remarks still true today? Have institutional researchers had an influence on higher education? Have institutional researchers had any effect on the thinking about higher education?

At this stage of its development, the field of institutional research may point with modest pride to a few obvious successes. Perhaps the most significant of these is the collection and analysis of institutional data. As a field, it has achieved a relatively high degree of sophistication in the collection and analysis of data dealing with student enrollments, space utilization, faculty work loads, costs, and other information needed for planning and management. Success in the collection and analysis of data points to success in the development of methodologies for institutional management and administrative decision making. We have come a long way in developing quantitative applications for higher education. True, we can be faulted for not developing sufficient qualitative institutional research methods, but higher education in general has not dealt adequately with the entire issue of quality.

Critics also argue that we have been able to compile volumes of facts and figures but have not succeeded in having that information used in the decision-making process. The central thrust of the managerial revolution, which Rourke and Brooks described years ago, has involved the information revolution in which few would deny we now find ourselves. But will we move from the mere collection and analysis of data to full utilization of our informational resources in decision making and policy setting? Will we see an explosion of information of a different type, as today's rapidly developing technology filters its way down to higher education, to administrative desks, and into policy and practices?

By and large, institutional researchers have been sensitive to the changing demands society has placed on our institutions of higher learning. But, sensitivity is not enough in the present environment of revenue shortfalls and enrollment declines. If it is to remain a viable entity in higher education, institutional research must develop better techniques to anticipate problems and changes, and to communicate that information in the policy arena. No longer can we rely on the old methods and concepts of institutional adaptation. There is a need to formulate an awareness of change that is systematic, critical and innovative.

In the future, the planning function must receive special attention from the institutional researcher. In the past, some institutional researchers have been reluctant to accept the responsibilities of planning. But this must change. As early as 1970, Saupe and Montgomery wrote that planning was closely associated with institutional research: "Perhaps long-range planning should become the focal point for institutional research efforts. It may not be too extreme to suggest that the influential research organizations of the future will be those that are concerned with planning and constantly test the probable effects of pending decisions" (p. 11). This has never been more true than in today's environment. Because of the data and analysis at his disposal, the institutional researcher can be one of the most knowledgeable individuals in an institution about that institution's future direction.

Any institutional planning effort requires information on the institution's past, its present situation, its environment, and forecasts of its future condition. But those who plan—that is, the institution's major decision makers—must have this information and these analyses in a timely and relevant manner. In other words, they need quality management information in order to plan and decide the institution's future. Institutional researchers should fill this role. In fact, we would argue that they *must* fill this role in the institutional planning process if institutional research is to remain a viable administrative specialty.

As argued before in this volume, the role of institutional researchers in the formulation of policy and planning certainly includes an involvement in politics in order to achieve the desired goals and objectives. Since so many of the decisions involving colleges and universities in the private and the public sectors are political, it is almost a necessity that institutional research officers play an active role in the political struggles that directly affect their institutions.

In the current decade, institutions are and will be faced with a set of problems different from those they have faced before. Changing demographic patterns have altered the pool of the traditional college-going age group. Institutions are reaching out for nontraditional, adult learners. Graduate study, particularly at the doctoral level, is decreasing at many campuses. The sagging economy is producing report after report of state and institutional cutbacks, financial exigency, program closings, and staff layoffs. Retrenchment, rather than growth, is the watchword.

In this environment, institutional research officers must assist institutional executives as they attempt to solve these critical problems. They must help their institutions prepare for the challenges of the future. An analysis of alternative policy changes will be very helpful, especially if accompanied by thoughtful, interpretive comments from an individual or office that has a reputation for thorough understanding of the characteristics and dynamics of the institution. Such involved, influential institutional research involves politics in its purest sense.

But one must remember Tetlow's pragmatic imperative. Decisions are rarely made in a totally rational manner. The situational context of the decision may not be conducive to the rational approach. Not all of the information available to a decision maker will be used in the decision. Finally, the decision maker's personality, decision style, facility with information, and relationship with the institutional researcher all affect the degree to which the results of the institutional researcher's work will be used in decision making.

These notions are of course a far cry from traditional institutional research values, which argue that institutional research should remain aloof from decision making. Unfortunately, such institutional research remains tangential to the main processes of the institution. Its products are received, seldom utilized, and relegated to the shelf to gather dust — or worse, to be discarded. In today's environment there is little room for functions, offices, or individuals whose outputs are peripheral to the main processes of institutions. On a campus where the financial prospects are grim, if the products of institutional research are not being utilized, if the institutional research office is not valued or productive, if the institutional researchers are not in the mainstream of the institution's policy and planning process, a decision may very likely be made that the resources needed to produce those products, support that office, and pay those staff can best be used in other ways. In sum, if institutional research is not perceived as being an essential function, it may cease to be a function at all.

References

Cohen, M. D., and March, J. G. *Leadership and Ambiguity: The American College President.* New York: McGraw-Hill, 1974.

Jones, D. P. *Data and Information for Executive Decisions in Higher Education.* Boulder, Colo.: National Center for Higher Education Management Systems, 1982.

Mayhew, L. B. "Imperatives for Institutional Research." A paper delivered at the Sixth Annual Forum of the Association for Institutional Research, Boston, May 1966.

Rourke, F. E., and Brooks, G. E. *The Managerial Revolution in Higher Education.* Baltimore, Md.: Johns Hopkins University Press, 1966.

Saupe, J. L., and Montgomery, J. R. *The Nature and Role of Institutional Research — Memo to a College or University.* Tallahassee, Fla.: Association for Institutional Research, 1970.

William F. Lasher is associate vice president for budget and institutional studies at the University of Texas at Austin and is immediate past president of the Association for Institutional Research.

James W. Firnberg is assistant vice president for academic affairs and director of institutional research for the Louisiana State University System. He is also professor of educational research at Louisiana State University, Baton Rouge.

Index

A

Action research, role of, 27-28
Administrative style, in environmental scan, 29-31
Advisory Committee on Intergovernmental Relations, 78, 79, 83, 87
Albright, A. D., 53, 60, 62
American Association of State Colleges and Universities, 51, 62
American College Testing (ACT) program, 59
American Council on Education, 81
Andersen, C. J., 21, 24
Arts and Humanities Foundation, 81
Association of American Universities (AAU), 45, 81; Data Exchange Network of, 47
Association of Collegiate Registrars, 80

B

Balderston, F. E., 26, 36
Baldridge, J. V., 5, 8, 9, 26, 36
Belkin, N. J., 5, 9
Big Eight, 45, 47-48
Bloom, A. M., 48
Bogue, E. G., 2, 49-62, 94-95
Brooks, G. E., 89, 97, 99
Buhl, L. C., 27-28, 36
Bureau of Education, 78
Bureau of Labor Statistics, 81
Bureau of the Budget, 81

C

California, planning in, 21
California at Berkeley, University of, and study of higher education, 84
California Postsecondary Education Commission, 21, 24
Caplan, N., 17, 24
Carnegie Foundation for the Advancement of Teaching, 64, 66, 75
Census Bureau, 19, 81, 82
Civil Rights Act of 1964, 84
Cohen, D. K., 17, 24
Cohen, M. D., 29, 36, 37, 91, 99
Coleman report, 22, 84
Cooperative Research Act of 1954, 83
Council for the Advancement of Small Colleges (CASC), 45
Cowley, W. H., 7, 9
Cox, G., 80
Curtis, D. V., 36

D

Data: comparisons of, 39-48; defined, 90; information distinct from, 12-14; processing of, 13-14
Data exchange: choosing institutions for, 45; gathering data for, 44; mechanism for, 42-45; nature of, 41-42; networks for, 43; one-way, 42-43; peer groups for, 45-48; politics of, 39-48; reasons for, 40-41; role of, 95-96; scope of, 43-44; two-way, 43; uses of, 39-40
Dearman, N. B., 21, 24
Decision making: alternative views of, 8; context of, 5-6; and institutional research, 68-72; macro, 68, 69-70; micro, 69, 70-72; rationality in, 6-7, 91-92
Decision structures, in environmental scan, 31-32
Dressel, P., 26-27, 37

E

Ecker, G., 36
Education Commission of the States (ECS), 20
Educational Amendments Act of 1972, 21, 84
Educational Amendments of 1974, 81
Educational Resources Information Center (ERIC), 16, 25-26, 84
Eiden, L. J., 21, 24
Elementary and Secondary Education Act of 1965, 84
Elliot, P. G., 50, 51, 62

101

Elsass, J. E., 45, 48
Elton, C. F., 45, 48
Enarson, H., 50, 62
Environmental scan, steps in, 29-33, 91-92
Evaluation, politics of, 22-23

F

Federal government: future support by, 86; and institutional research, 77-87; and research about higher education, 83-87; role of, 93-94; and statistics, 78-83
Feldman, M. S., 3-4, 5-6, 9
Fincher, C. L., 1-2, 11-24, 90, 92
Finn, C. E., Jr., 78, 87
Firnberg, J. W., 1-2, 89-100
Folger, J., 2, 77-87, 93
Folsom, M., 80
Frankel, M. M., 21, 24
Fund for the Improvement of Postsecondary Education, 20

G

Georgia, planning in, 21
Gerald, D. E., 21, 24
GI Bill of 1944, 77, 78
Gladieaux, L., 78, 87
Governor's Committee on Postsecondary Education, 21, 24
Grant, W. V., 21, 24

H

Haas, R. M., 28, 37
Hartmark, L. S., 37, 48
Harvard, and early institutional research, 7
Hatch Act of 1887, 78
Health Professions Education Assistance Act, 77
Higher Education Act of 1965, 81
Higher Education Facilities Act of 1963, 81
Higher Education General Information Survey (HEGIS), 19, 44, 79, 82, 93
Hines, E. R., 25-26, 37
Hoyt, D. P., 45, 48

I

Information: conclusions on, 23-24; control of, 35; data distinct from, 12-14; defined, 5; and institutional research, 90-91; interpretation of, 91; knowledge distinct from, 14-15; political pressures for, 15-17; political uses of, 17-19; politics of, 11-24; processing styles for, 17-18; strength of, 34-35; as sympathetic magic, 11; technology and, 18-19; utilization of, 3-5
Institute for Educational Leadership, 78, 87
Institutional research: active role for, 28; and decision making, 68-72; defined, 3, 78; developing political strategy for, 34-36; effectiveness of, 27; and environmental scan, 29-33; and federal government, 77-87; and federal statistics, 78-83; future of, 89-100; history of, 7, 30-31, 92-93; impact of, 96-97; and information, 90-91; institutionalization of, 7; issues for, 35-36; and planning, 98-99; politicization of, 5; pragmatic imperative of, 3-10; role of, 26-28; and self-assessment, 33-34; and state agencies, 63-75; strategic planning for, 29-34; trends in, 89-90
Institutions: community support for, 58-59; data exchange by, 39-48; management competence and integrity in, 57-58; as political, 25-26; politics within, 25-37; and proposal timing and completeness, 56-57; research about, 83-87; responsibilities of, 65-66; and state agencies, 49-75; statutory roles of, 64-68

J

Jencks, C., 26, 37
Jones, D. P., 4, 5, 9, 99

K

Kansas, University of (KU), and peer group data exchange, 45-48
Kansas Board of Regents, 48
Keen, P. G. W., 8, 9
Key actors, in environmental scam, 32-33
Knowledge, information distinct from, 14-15

L

Land Grant College Acts, 78
Land Grant College Association, 81

Lasher, W. F., 1-2, 89-100
Lawrence, G. B., 5, 9
Lindblom, C., 17, 24
Lindquist, J., 27-28, 36
Lingenfelter, P. E., 2, 45, 48, 63-75, 94-95
Livingston, J. S., 53, 62
Lorang, W. G., Jr., 48
Louisiana, state agency in, 59
Louisiana State University, and state agency, 59

M

McCoy, M., 45, 48
McGuiness, A., 78, 87
Management: competence and integrity in, 57-58; politics of, 21-22
Management by objectives (MBO), 21-22
Management information systems (MIS), 21-22
March, J. G., 3-4, 5-6, 9, 29, 36, 37, 91, 99
Martin, R. O., 45, 48
Mayhew, L. B., 97, 99
Millett, J., 26, 37
Montgomery, J. R., 27, 37, 48, 98, 99
Mood, A., 81
Morrison, A., 17, 24
Morton, M. S. S., 8, 9

N

National Association for State Universities and Land Grant Colleges (NASULGC), 45
National Association of College Business Officers, 80-81
National Center for Education Statistics (NCES), 16, 21, 79, 81-83, 87, 94
National Center for Higher Education Management Systems (NCHEMS), 20; major research universities Task Force of, 45, 46-47
National Commission on Financing Postsecondary Education, 84
National Defense Education Act of 1958, 77, 81
National Institute of Education (NIE), 20, 81, 85
National Science Foundation, 78, 79
National Teacher Examination, 59
North Carolina, higher education laboratory in, 84

O

Office of Education, 78, 80, 81, 83-85
Office of Management and Budget (OMB), 42, 82, 83
Ohio State University, vocational education center at, 84

P

Parsons, T., 26, 37
Peer groups, for data exchange, 45-48
Planning: and institutional research, 98-99; politics of, 20-21
Planning, programming, budgeting systems (PPBS), 21-22
Platt, G. M., 37
Plisko, V. W., 21, 24
Politics: of data exchange, 39-48; defined, 1, 25-26, 49; of evaluation, 22-23; of information, 11-24; in institutions, 25-37; of management, 21-22; of planning, 20-21; small p and capital P types of, 69; of state agencies, 49-75

R

Rawson, T. M., 45, 48
Riesman, D., 26, 37
Riley, G. L., 36
Rosenthal, R., 53, 62
Rourke, F. E., 89, 97, 99
Russell, J. D., 90

S

Sabatler, P., 6, 9
Sanford, N., 90
Sanford, T., 66
Saunders, L. E., 2, 25-37, 91-92
Saupe, J. L., 3, 9, 27, 37, 54, 62, 98, 99
Scroggs, S., 7, 9
Service, A. L., 5, 9
Shirley, R. C., 48
Shulman, C. H., 79, 87
Simon, H. A., 8, 9
Smart, J. C., 45, 48
Smith-Lever Act of 1914, 78
Southern Regional Education Board (SREB), 20
Southern University, and state agency, 59
Sproull, L., 78, 84, 85, 87
Stambaugh, R. J., 17, 24
State agencies: as adversaries or advo-

cates, 56-60; boundary role of, 50-53; and budget formulas, 71-72; and candor, 54-55; and compromise, 55; and creative tension, 55; and decision-making process, 68-72; future of, 60-61; and institutional research, 63-75; institutional view of, 49-62; issues for, 51-53, 61; legislative and executive, 67-68; and planning, 21; politics of, 49-75; and pressure for information, 15, 94-95; proposals and personalities in, 57; relationships with, 53-56, 72-74; and respect, 55-56; responsibilities of, 66-67

T

Teeter, D. J., 2, 39-48, 96
Terenzini, P. T., 45, 48
Tetlow, W. L., 1, 3-10, 90-91, 92, 99
Thornton, R., 58, 62

V

Vail, C., 53, 56, 60, 62

W

Walker, D. E., 5. 9
Walker, H., 80
Weiner, S., 78, 84, 85, 87
Western Interstate Commission on Higher Education, 84
Wilensky, H. L, 18, 24
Wolanin, T., 78, 87
Wolf, D., 78, 84, 85, 87

Y

Yale, and early institutional research, 7

Z

Zero-based budgeting (ZBB), 21-22